Wurzels' World

Mervyn Hancock

WESTERN
Daily Press

Acknowledgments

Tommy and Pete would like to convey their thanks to each and every musician—too many to mention individually—who have given them their support at various times and especially to John and Jai with whom they are currently experiencing some of the most exciting gigs of their lengthy career, but no group of musicians can express themselves fully unless they have the backing of and complete confidence in their sound and road crew and this is all handled expertly by Leon, Glenn and DD(Dynamic Driver) Tony. Thanks lads you do a brilliant job. After the tragic death of Adge, it is thanks to John Miles for his never ending enthusiasm, drive, encouragement and superb Management which took them to the dizzy heights of No1 in the Music Charts, only to be followed by some rather lean years when there was even talk of them finishing. Therefore they fully appreciate the important role that a certain Paul Gunningham played in the late 90's when he badgered EMI into re-issuing some Wurzel tracks, resulting in the release of "The finest 'Arvest of the Wurzels". At various times throughout the years the lads were supported by other first class West Country musicians—amongst them, on bass Ron Keys, on keyboards Terry Pascoe and Paul Buck, and for many years musical director Rod Owen (a Rovers Supporter to boot) and on drums-pre John-Bill Pinnell. Many thanks lads.

EMI's Steve Woof then introduced the boys to Sil Willcox, who when asked if he would like to manage them, instantly agreed to do so. Here was the Manager for whom they had waited and desperately needed for so many years—to get them back in the recording studio, releasing records again and making the public aware that they were still very much alive and kicking. He sure has done that, and made the past couple of years possibly their most successful to date. On the recording front they have been pushed and cajoled by the effervescent, highly inventive Louie Nicastro, their loopy recording engineer. He has worked for so long with Sil that he is every bit as enthusiastic and mad as Sil, is an absolute delight to work with in the studio and it would appear from their last couple of albums that he gets the best from them. Keep up the good work, Louie, they love being bullied by you. Thanks, Sil, you are champion.

Moreover, Tommy and Pete would like to thank the many fans who have supported them through thick and thin, and they welcome all the new ones who have recently discovered them and who, with Sil's massive contribution, have resurrected their career and extended their shelf life beyond all of their dreams. Thanks, you've done a proper job!

Wurzels' World

Contents

4	Cutler of the West
14	The Show Must Go On
19	The only Scottish Wurzel in Captivity
23	Pete Budd's tales from the Riverbank
29	The Early Years
49	John Morgan on the Forest Beat
51	Wurzel Jai had a cracking job
54	"I wish I was Back on the Farm..."
58	Wurzelgate
61	The West is Wurzelised in Song
66	The Wurzels' fans and mates!
	Extra Wurzels
72	Ready, Steady Cook
73	Wurzels in colour
91	West Country Hall of Fame
104	What is Cider?
106	Wurzel Recipes
113	Wurzel Songs & Speak

Chapter 1

Cutler of the West

It all started with a fiver, a visit to a pawn shop and some funny hats...Back in 1966.

A voice roared down the corridor of power at the famous Abbey Road studios in London's St John's Wood.
EMI boss Sir Joseph Lockwood was on the warpath.
This was the hallowed studios where The Beatles had recorded their smash-hit records, and where the Mersey sound was being immortalised.
"Why are there straw bales spilling across the pavements?" he demanded.
"How did those four tramps get past security?"
"What is that unholy row coming from Studio Number 2?" Studio Two was the very place which had only just been vacated by George, John, Paul and Ringo!
The boys from Bristol had arrived with their agent. The press had been alerted. Scrumpy and Western had come to Lunnun, a challenge was being made to the Fab Four, by the rustic four - Adge Cutler and the Wurzels.
Sir Joseph couldn't believe what he was seeing, or hearing...but by the end of the day his foot was tapping to something completely different than he was offered from the usual hopefuls.
Adge Cutler and his boys celebrated a new contract, in the local pub...with a few pints of cider!

Radios, record players and television sets were blasting out the Beatles' Number One hit song Paperback Writer back in June 1966.
This was the age of "Flower Power" – a time for romance, long hair, strange clothes, and exotic cocktails.
The Fab Four, with their mop haircuts, lapel-less coats, and Liverpudlian accents, seemed to be unstoppable.
Far away from Merseyside, back in Bristol, 36-year-old, unemployed, Alan John Cutler needed to make money!
A spell in his father's coach hire business in Nailsea, some time making cider for Mr Coates, then helping to build a power station in Wales, and finally a financially disastrous year in Spain, looking for property for development, had left him skint.Adge, as his drinking pals knew him, was born in Portishead, Somerset in 1930 (famous for a 90's band of the same name) and grew up in neighbouring Nailsea.

After leaving school at 14 and doing his National Service, he became Acker Bilks' road manager in 1960.
But in June 1966 he had the clothes he stood up in, a fiver in his pocket, and a collection of songs. The songs had already been well aired in local pubs, but now he needed to turn them into cash.
Through working with Acker, Adge had made friends with the owner of a well-known Bristol entertainment agency – The Miles Organisation.
He borrowed his bus fare, and set off to see John Miles, with a scheme to set up a comic band. If John, Paul, George and Ringo could make a fortune with the Mersey Sound, then why couldn't he hit the charts with a mixture of West Country humour and a bit of good old Bristol dialect?
After all, he explained at the time, this was the beginning of the so-called psychedelic era and if an American group called The Prunes, could hit the charts with "I had too much to dream last night" – acclaimed as one of the first songs of the emerging Garage Music – why not some farmyard tunes for local consumption.

Adge said at the time: "I gave my first public performance when I was about seven at the Village Institute, Nailsea. I sang 'There'll always be a Nailsea'. Being a regular Saturday-night-drinker I later noticed that it was usually songs about London or Glasgow that were being sung in the bars and that there was nothing local to sing. I thought a good roaring pub song, that's what they want. So I wrote 'Drink Up Thy Zider' about 1958 and the song just spread. Then I started writing songs about different villages and they passed into local history. I even travelled to Liverpool and sang at the Cavern Club for a couple of quid. That was the first time I ever sang professionally."

Adge did a detour and took his fiver down to Raselles, the Bristol Pawn Brokers in Old Market, and demanded to see the selection of clothes. Discarding anything that resembled fashion or the trend of the time, he carefully selected four different sized pairs of heavy-duty cord trousers. The very items that people from outside the West, associated with West Country yokels.Thick, granddad shirts, minus collars, waistcoats and neckerchiefs would be the "fashionable" accessories...he asked for, but didn't get, and change. But the delighted shopkeeper was glad to see the end of a pile of old rubbish, which he had intended to donate to the youngsters for their Guy Fawkes.

John Miles had an eye for the unusual, and could see a market for a group which offered a completely different style and presentation from the chart toppers of the time.

Agriculture was the main industry in the South West, and many young people in the area were still relying on Young Farmers' Dances for their first encounters with the opposite sex – music provided by local groups, and held in village halls.
If nothing else, a rustic group of hopefuls, singing songs that struck a cord with their audience, would bring in a few bob, and maybe just strike a cord with a record company.

There was some formidable competition mind you! Ike and Tina Turner with River Deep, Mountain High, Dusty Springfield's You Don't have to say you Love Me, The Troggs Wild Thing and The Kinks Sunny Afternoon all had their places in the charts.
John Miles agreed to manage Adge and sent him off to find a backing group." He's got the trousers, now he needed to fill them," he said.
Almost 40 years later, John still recalls the early days of trying to find work for the band.
"I had offices in Whiteladies Road, Bristol, and 350 pop groups on my books,"he said.
"Adge used to sit in my office when I used to call around clubs and other venues, and try to explain what the lads did. Most of them were quite bemused, and when someone actually said they would book them, I used to pretend to be looking through a diary to see if they were available. They actually had no work at all, and Adge used to see the funny side of this."
Adge contacted some pals from the local music (mainly jazz) scene.
He found jazz banjoist Reg Quantrill, accordion player Reg Chant, bass player John Macey and a kind of twisted tuba, later named the Wurzelphone, and played with dexterity by Brian Walker. Adge armed himself with a home-made walking stick" cut from the hedge near Nailsea.
All that was needed now was a name for weird collection of chaps in the backing group. They looked a bit like walking scarecrows, and they always had a head made from a turnip! The root vegetable's brother was a Mangelwurzel – grown for feeding to cattle, and also an endearing name for someone living south of Gloucester.
So Adge Cutler and the Wurzels was launched.

John Miles wasted no time in promoting his new signings. He recognised that some of Adge's local ditties were not only very funny, but carried a good tune, and would provide a light hearted break from the more serious, mainly love songs, being churned out by the established pop stars.
"I had a friend called Bob Barratt who worked for EMI, and who owed me a few favours," said John.
"I told him about Adge Cutler and the Wurzels, and he invited us up to Abbey Road Studios to see what the songs would sound like in a professional setting.
"I told the lads that we needed to make a good impression. We drove up in an old van and I told them to put a few bales of straw and some milk churns in the back.
"When we arrived we threw the straw and churns out onto the road, and everyone in the studios were looking out of the windows to see what all the fuss was about.Then of course, the chairman himself came to Studio Two, which was used by The Beatles, and showed an interest. I believe that is why we got a recording contract."
The first Cutler song collection – to be dubbed "Scrumpy and Western Music" by an ardent and loyal fan club – was mainly written by the great man himself, and (maybe unwittingly) provided a snapshot of life in rural Britain.
Every gardener, for instance, battling to grow prize vegetables and blooms, was plagued by cooch grass. You could throw weed killer on it, dig down until you hit rock, and even build a bonfire on the troublesome plant – but kill it? No way! Each year it would produce its white, strangling stem, and green shoots. Thee Cassent Kill Cooch – No Matter just how much thee's try crooned Adge, to a supportive crowd of extremely well oiled fans at the Royal Oak Nailsea on November 2 1966.

I had just celebrated my 19th birthday, was employed as a young journalist on the Devon and Somerset News in Tiverton, Devon, and was writing a pop column, when I received an invitation to the live cutting of an album by the giant EMI recording company. We were to arrive there in the early afternoon, and would then be introduced to, and given the opportunity to interview their latest star.

No one in the office – or any surrounding offices as far as I could gather – had heard of Adge Cutler. But EMI were big stuff, with some of the top names in their stable, and invitations to recording sessions, were few and far between. Record producer Bob Barratt was the contact at the pub, where sound recordists, and an odd selection of the good and great, mainly from the Bristol area, or customers and contacts of John Miles, joined regular customers.

Even for a lad born and bred in Devon, the strangely dressed group of men in one corner of the pub, were rustic to the extreme. One was snorting snuff up his nose, and sneezing with great gusto. Another was tackling a mug of cider, which had been handed to him by a photographer.

Locals explained that the cider would become significant later in the evening, when the apple of Adge's collection (so to speak) Drink Up Thee Zider would almost raise the roof of the ancient Inn.

Rules were laid out for the entertainment. This was to be a live recording, and so audience sounds were needed – but silence would be maintained during the songs, but plenty of appreciative applause and shouting would enhance proceedings between each of the offerings. Brian Walker recalls: 'I remember that there was lots of free cider flowing, well I can remember the first half of the recording anyway'.

Adge himself would introduce some of the tunes – those not born in the South West would seek an interpreter later.

No one knew on that evening, in the smoke-filled bar, that the very first song Twice Daily would later incur the wrath of the BBC and be banned from the airwaves.

For us the words were very funny, and not in the least offensive. For the hierarchy at Broadcasting House, they were full of sexy innuendos, and most unsatisfactory to be heard by the populace at large.

In fact, news of the ban, was later to make it one of the most requested records of the day, and help Drink up Thee Zider climb to 45 in the UK charts when it was released as a double sided single.

Adge had already given his mandatory interviews, explaining that his mustard-coloured waistcoat was designed to cover up the snuff stains, and the corduroy trousers were ideal for windy days on the Mendip Hills, rather than a fashion statement.

Some hacks were already casting scorn on the group's hopes for stardom. "Do you think you can topple the Beatles, and have girls screaming at you," said one, with a knowing wink to the rest of us.

"We already bin screamed at," replied Adge, unabashed, and laying on his Somerset dialect with a trowel "Twice in fact! First when old Reg there dropped his banjo on a woman's foot, and later when my ferret poked his head out of my trousers to see what was going on."

The mood was set, long before the sound recordists gave the thumbs up, and Bob Barratt climbed up onto the stage, and said: "Ladies and Gentlemen, Present Cider Mugs for the Pride of Priddy – Adge Cutler and the Wurzels."

It might have been a sound only event for the thousands who would eventually buy the record – but for the audience that night, Adge and his group spared no efforts in giving them a visual feast. Scrumpy and Western was launched onto the unsuspecting nation.

The songs on the first album Adge Cutler and the Wurzels (Columbia SX6126) were not only classics, which are still sung in pubs and clubs to this day, but were also very funny and topical stories, put to music.
Few ordinary people understood, or indeed cared about, the Common Market, or what effect it would have on them. Euro-MPs and the prospect of a super Parliament in Brussels, would obviously have a profound affect on businessmen and particularly the farming industry, in later years.
But in 1966 the EU was far away from towns and villages in the South West...except one!

Adge put his innovative mind and great sense of humour to imagining how it might be received in the area in which he grew up. What would happen When The Common Market Comes to Stanton Drew?
Not many people outside of Somerset or Bristol had heard of Stanton Drew. But Adge soon changed all that.

> "When George comes home from milking, he'll get a big surprise,
> when he sits down expecting Irish Stew.
> "And his wife says George I'll get'ee, a girt dollop of spaghetti, 'cos
> the Common Market's come to Stanton Drew."

Those words made everyone smile. Pasta was yet to become a fashionable meal for skinny young things.
"Most people around here have only seen spaghetti in a tin, and no matter how long they boil it, the tin stays as hard as a rock," Adge explained.
"I saw a girt big tank, of Portuguese Vin Blanc, parked in Pensford High Street t'other night," the song continued – immortalising another town. The birthplace and home of his friend and former employer, the legendary Acker Bilk.

The Chew Magna Cha-cha-cha - a take off of some of the weirder dances that were around at the time, had magnificent rhythm, and a chance for the boys to twirl around on the stage.

If the music didn't warm the audience, then the sight of Reg "Snake hips" Quantrill – the Elvis Presley of Chewton Mendip – writhing around in his farming attire, sent many women (and men) into hysterics.

In the mid-60s youngsters could choose their careers – jobs were plentiful. Most aspired to become white-collar workers, but Adge saw his own father in a fictional role as The Champion Dung Spreader.
As a lad he would have seen farmhands engaged in the awesome, and dirty job, of spreading animal manure around the fields, using a pitchfork.
It is improbable that 'When dad was in his power, with a mighty two-arm swipe, he hit the old church tower. My goodness, said the vicar, has the judgement come? No sir, said the curate, 'tis a hundredweight of dung!'.

If the record was going to make an impact – and sell a lot of copies – then the biggest centre of population, Bristol, would provide many of the customers. So Adge didn't forget the capital city of the West. Inspired by the Bristol motto – Virtute Et Industrial – the Wurzels took a swipe at the Bristol dialect, making sure the two soccer teams, Rovers and City, got a good mention!
Now we be Bristol kiddays, we comes from Bristol Cittay, where all the boys is 'ansome, and all the girls is prettay – the locals loved it.
I also loved it. Inspired by memories of that night in the Royal Oak, I decided that Adge should be introduced to the good people of Tiverton, Devon, where I worked.

In 1967 I booked Adge Cutler and the Wurzels at the Tiverton Motel. I got a package deal, which included up and coming comedian/folksinger Fred Wedlock and songstress Joan O'Brien.
I remember paying the fee of £125 to the John Miles Organisation (I was earning about £12 a week at the time) and booking the Motel, and praying I could find enough people to part with 15shillings each (75p) to cover my costs.
The place was packed, and I went away with a small profit!

I had another encounter with Adge and his Wurzels in 1968, when I was the public relations officer at Butlins Holiday Camp in Minehead.
Radio One Club had decided to take to the road, and Alan Freeman was the DJ in charge when the boys appeared to sing.
They went down a storm with 10,000 people in the audience, and later Adge agreed to pose for publicity pictures next to the "Mad Mouse" – a kind of roller coaster which soared above the chalets.

Adge, who had a fear of heights, agreed to sit on one of the coaster cars, provided it didn't move! Someone gave it a shove and set it going – Adge emerged some six minutes later, as white as a sheet, after his unscheduled ride into the sky.
Adge and his group were in great demand, and he had cash in his pocket. But although the group was set to sing its way through four decades, Wurzelling was not a career that would suit everyone, and Wurzels would vanish, and be replaced by other hopefuls.
Brian Walker would be the first to retire – his undoubted talents on the Wurzelphone left a void in the group. Henry Davis arrived in 1967 to take over the Wurzelphone, followed by Melt Kingston then Henry returned for a short spell and was replaced by Tony Baylis.

Since Tony left in the early 80s there has been a succession of bass players starting with Jai Howe to Mike Gwilliam to Dave Wintour and now back to Jai. When Adge's right hand man, Reg Quantrill decided to leave the group in 1973, fans thought it would be the greatest loss of all......but four years later tragedy struck. Some of the words from his immortal cider drinkers' anthem were to come true!

"Drink up thee zider George, thee bissn't goin ' far"

Adge had been trying to shake off a cold during a week at The Crystal Room in Hereford, where he and the Wurzels had played to capacity audiences.
He told his group members that he intended to go home and rest before finalising arrangements with his agent for a television series and a new album. This was to be the big one, the breakthrough.
Adge Cutler and the Wurzels had been a West Country attraction for some time, but their fame was spreading, and they were on the verge of national success. But on Sunday May 5 1974, Alan John Cutler, one of three sons born to Jack and Dorothy Cutler, probably fell asleep at the wheel of his sports car. It flipped over and he was trapped underneath. He was dead by the time the ambulance arrived. The West Country was in shock.
Pete Budd, guitarist and banjo player with the band, recalled how he had been due to pick up the boss and drive him to and from the gig.
"We both had sports cars, and I told me dad that I was giving Adge a lift, but the plans were changed at the last minute," he said.
"We all made our own way home from Hereford, and I arrived in the early hours of the morning and went to bed.

"The next day I called in at the local for a drink, and the atmosphere was strange and quiet.
"One of the blokes said: 'You haven't had the news yet, have you? Adge Cutler was killed in a car crash earlier today.
"I just shook my head in disbelief – I thought I was in the middle of a dream. I called John Miles and he confirmed the news.
"Adge was not only the lead singer for the group, he was a very old friend. I knew him at the time when he formed the Wurzels.
"Then I thought – Oh God! My dad probably thinks I was in the car, and I rushed off to tell him that I was OK"

Adge's untimely death was reported throughout the local and national press.The Bristol Evening Post (May 6 1974) ran its tribute under the banner headline - "KING ADGE DIES IN CRASH, BUT.......WE'LL PLAY ON, SAY THE WURZELS - Adge Cutler, King of Scrumpy and Western music, died at the weekend in a car crash. But, his group, The Wurzels, will continue with Adge's music, their agent, Mr John Miles pledged that afternoon. It was one of Adge's wishes that his songs would continue after his death."

A Coroner's court heard how the star was returning home in the early hours of the morning, from Hereford when his sports car overturned at Newhouse roundabout, near Chepstow, on the approach to the Severn Bridge. No other vehicle was involved.
The car struck a bollard, hit the kerb, and overturned on the roundabout.
He was just a short distance from his home at Tickenham Hill, Tickenham.
Adge Cutler, who was 44, left a wife Yvonne. They were married two years earlier.
Adge, who took his nickname from the sound of his initials – AJ - was the son of a motor cycle, taxi and coach hire firm owner from Nailsea.
After leaving school he worked as a market gardener and then joined his father's business. He went into the music business at the end of the 1950s when he became road manager to Acker Bilk.

Adge spent four years on the road with the Bilk band, and then quit to live in Spain for a year, where he searched out development sites for a property company. The venture was not a success, and he returned to the West Country. Adge Cutler and the Wurzels were formed, and started appearances in June 1966.

He was an immediate success in the West Country, and his first record "Drink Up Thee Zider" sold 100,000 copies and established him as a nationally known singer. He was booked solidly, and his engagements included a coast-to-coast appearance on Canadian Television.

Mr Miles said in a moving tribute to his star: "One of Adge's greatest wishes was that the songs he had written about Bristol and this area would continue to be sung after his death, in pubs and anywhere they would be enjoyed.
"We shall continue the Wurzels to do just that, but obviously the personal humour everyone loved in Adge will not be there anymore.
"It is a great tragedy and it comes at a time when Adge was about to make the final breakthrough to the Continent and elsewhere."

Ten years later the Western Daily Press recorded the anniversary of his death with a feature called "SO DRINK UP THEE ZIDER......AND TOAST OLD ADGE".
Reporter David Stuckey said: "He may not have been the greatest entertainer to come out of the West, but his enthusiasm and enjoyment, especially of the North Somerset scene, was infectious.
"And behind that yokel exterior lurked a talent that wanted so much to say something meaningful about the changing rural scene, the disappearing countryside, the Avon-fied rape of Bristol...Adge wanted to achieve something lasting and meaningful."

Chapter 2

The Show Must Go On

"When I got the call on that Sunday morning, to say that Adge was dead, I felt completely devastated. He was not only a lovely chap but also a great friend. I telephoned the boys in the band – they were still in bed. I spoke to Tommy Banner, one of the Wurzels, and he just didn't want to go on. I told them that if they continued as a group I would get them a Number One hit. A year or so later we were on Top of the Pops, at number one, with COMBINE HARVESTER" – John Miles, former Wurzels' agent.

Wurzels come and Wurzels go, but two faces have always dominated the group from its early days – accordion player Tommy Banner and guitarist Pete Budd. And it was up to them whether or not the group would continue without their front man.

"Adge was irreplaceable, but we did at least have someone who was a very good front man – and that was Pete Budd," said Tommy.
In fact, just like Tommy Banner - who had been totally amazed at being asked to come down from his native Scotland, dress up in funny clothes, and sing daft songs – the other long standing Wurzel was an accomplished rock and roller! Pete Budd and the Rebels were an established group in the West during the early 1960s.
The other group member facing the prospect of continuing as a trio, was Tony Baylis, a young Londoner, who was still trying to come to terms with his OoooohhAArs!
John Miles recalls that bookings did falter after Adge's funeral, which was attended by some 1,500 people.
Many people thought that without their leader, the group would simply disappear. No one could contemplate trying to find another Adge......there was no one like him anyway!
Pete Budd said: "We were all devastated, but John brought us back to earth, and said that we still had a living to make.
"We didn't know whether the group had a future without Adge, and then there were all the bookings – we wondered if people would want us without Adge.

"Anyway we booked the Globe Inn at Newton St Loe, and played solidly there for a week.
"We fulfilled all our outstanding bookings and people were marvellous.
"I took over as lead singer, and the biggest problem was making sure I knew all the words of the songs.
"I did know most of them, but it was a case of learn the others as we went along."

Almost two years after the Wurzels took the road alone, John Miles came across an advertising agency that was trying to dream up a new way to sell cream. Various actors, groups, catchphrases and jingles had been tried out, but none seem to hit the mark.

The Wurzels simply came up with the expression: "Give 'em a gert big dollop." They got the contract, and their faces were on the television in 30-second bursts, in the middle of some of the biggest and most popular television series of the time.
"The phrase seemed to catch the mood of that summer," said John Miles.
But something even bigger was to catch the attention of music fans of all ages and from all backgrounds.

A young lady called Melanie had been singing a song called Brand New Key which was quite daft, but had a catchy tune.
The Wurzels found an even dafter subject, a Combine Harvester and changed the words, and came up with a massive hit.
The song, which told the tale of a country fella, trying to get his hands on a wench's (wait for it) bit of land, was being sung in clubs, pubs, aired on the radio, and selling records like hot cakes.
It raced to number one, and the lads found themselves in London, appearing on Top of the Pops.

Tommy Banner recalls how other groups arrived in the studios carrying bags full of trendy costumes, while they had their corduroy trousers, collarless shirts and neckerchiefs.
"I was taken to a room where I had my hair washed, and a young lady was blow drying it when the door burst open, and there was Les McKeown of the Bay City Rollers, who were very big in those days," recalled Tommy.
"We were taking prime position on the show, and he didn't appear to like it very much.

"He exploded! He said, 'We're supposed to be the pretty boys with the blow-dried hair, not you!' and he messed up my hair. 'You're supposed to be wurzels.'"

Journalist James Belsey from the Bristol Evening Post, recalled how the group changed as a direct result of that remark.

"The Wurzels honed and honed their act to slick perfection," he wrote.

"They'd abandoned the farmyard and scrumpy, and now inhabited a night-clubby world of gin'n Jags.

"Tony Baylis left and replacements followed.

"Pete Budd took over a pub in Devon and combined his work as a licensee and musician. Tommy Banner moved from Portishead to Taunton – and after 21 years, John Miles and the Wurzels parted company."

John, who said this year that he will "never retire" after 46 years of being in the entertainment business, recalls the parting.

"It was very amicable. I had given the lads what I promised, a Number One, but they were doing a lot of local gigs around the West Country, and needed someone to look after just them.

"I still love the Wurzels, often think of dear old Adge, and would help them all I could to this day."

In fact many people will remember the Wurzels hitting the big time, because many of them got a real bargain when the lads appeared in their local pub. Fame didn't go to their heads, and they insisted on fulfilling all their engagements at the agreed price – often at around £100 a night, when they were television and recording stars, who could have commanded so much more.

Tommy Banner is an ardent Bristol City fan, and believes that fellow soccer enthusiasts helped him put the group back on the right track after the Bay City Rollers affair.

The scene was Wembley Stadium, when City won the Freight Rover Trophy.

"Someone started singing Drink Up Thy Zider," he said. "The song began to spread along the terraces until it was all around Wembley. Businessmen in the expensive seats, the ordinary fans – everyone knew that song of Adge.

"I thought to myself – that's our strength, that's what we're about. Maybe we'd made a mistake turning into a cabaret act."

So the Wurzels became "scruffy" and "loveable" again – putting the same time and effort into gigs at student clubs, pubs, private parties, even wedding receptions, as they did with their television and radio appearances.

Many more songs were added to their repertoire, but the lads found that everyone still wanted the original hits they had made with Adge.
"You wouldn't believe that youngsters would know or love the Cutler classics so much," said Tommy. "But we've had to call extra security at student dates because they start invading the stage.
"We've even had to put together a medley of Adge's songs, because if we sang all the requests we'd be on stage for three hours."

*****

Where be that blackbird too, I know where 'ee be, 'ee be up yon Wurzel Tree and I be arter 'ee. 'Ee sees I, I sees 'e,e b*!*er if I won't gettun, wi' a girt big stick I'll knocun down, Blackbird I'll 'ave 'ee.

No one has quite figured out why North American folk should be entranced by a song about a yokel's bid to rid himself of a rook – but the Canadians were!
The Blackbird song flew to number one in the Canadian hit parade, and in February 1977, the lads flew off too, for a tour of the country.
Apparently in Newfoundland, Nova Scotia, Ottawa and Toronto, locals couldn't wait to get their hands on other Wurzel discs, especially Combine Harvester and I am a Zider drinker.
They certainly came down to earth with a bump the following month – providing a supporting act for the then Prime Minister, James Callaghan, when he opened a television studio in Manchester.

In 1977 Tommy was able to help boost the finances of Bristol City FC when the club decided to officially adopt one of the group's songs One for the Bristol City as their official theme tune.
An initial pressing of 20,000 copies of the record were snapped up by fans, and the club got 28p for each one.

By 1978 Wurzelmania had spread to the Middle East, and the boys were also appearing on networked television shows like That's Life, Seaside Special, Crackerjack, Cheggers, and the Basil Brush Show!
In June 1982 they discovered they had another fan in no less a person than Pope John Paul the Second.
The Wurzels received a personal message of thanks from the Pope for entertaining the crowds at Canterbury during his visit.
Less than 24 hours before the Pope was due for his historic meeting with the Archbishop of Canterbury, the group received an urgent call to go to entertain the waiting multitude.

They made their way to and from the city with a special police escort – the ecclesiastical gig had been squeezed in between bookings in Chippenham and Sturminster Newton.
John Miles said: "It was realised that the thousands of people who had turned up to see the Pope's arrival by helicopter, would have a long wait to see his departure again.
"So the church authorities decided to lay on entertainment. The Wurzels were on stage before this huge audience for about 25 minutes, and were performing when the Pope returned from seeing the Archbishop.
"He picked up the microphone and thanked them for keeping the crowds amused, and for making his visit to Canterbury an added pleasure.
"Then he blessed them – and for Tommy, who is a Catholic, it was a very moving occasion."

In fact the group wonders whether they received some help from even higher up in the heavens in July 1991, when they almost died in an incident on the M2 Motorway near Margate.
Tommy Banner was driving their Mercedes van at 70mph when a tyre burst and sent them careering across three lanes, back again, and ended up on a bank.
"It was very close, and we all thought we were going to die," said Tommy.
"There was a van behind us and they saw what was happening and held back. If they had hit us, that would have been the end of us all.
"The other van was carrying lads from a building site, and they stopped and helped us change the wheel, and shared some coffee from their Thermos flasks."

At Home with the man described by Adge Cutler as "The only Scottish Wurzel in Captivity" - veteran rocker TOMMY BANNER

"Tommy Banner is more than a talented accordion player with a whacky sense of humour. Behind the simple yokel image that is part of The Wurzels' famous live act lies a man of many dimensions."

You might expect that a Wurzel would live in the depths of rural Somerset, in a ramshackle farm cottage complete with its own cider press.
As befits the longest-serving member of Somerset's most famous musical export, Tommy does indeed live in the county with which The Wurzels are inextricably linked.
His home, however, is a smart, modern semi in a cul-de-sac in Taunton.
That is the first surprise. The second comes when Tommy starts speaking. For instead of speaking in a broad Somerset burr, his accent is distinctly Scottish.
Not so much "Oooh aar", as "Och aye".
Yet, as Tommy reveals: "You would be amazed at the number of people who meet me who are convinced I'm from Somerset.
"They associate The Wurzels with Somerset and don't seem to register that I speak with a Scottish accent. Maybe they think it's some strange Somerset dialect!" Tommy actually comes from the town of Penicuik, in the Mid-Lothian area of Scotland.

He came to Somerset in 1967 after getting a three-month contract to play accordion in a band called Adge Cutler and The Wurzels, which had just had a minor chart hit with a number called Drink Up Thy Cider.

"In those days there weren't many accordion players in the West Country, but there were plenty in Scotland and I was one of them, " he said.

"I thought it would just be a bit of fun. I'd never have guessed that I'd still be doing it 36 years later. I hadn't even tasted cider then."

Tommy's trademark is a mischievous smile and a mosaic of laughter lines spreads across his face whenever he recalls his years with the group.

It is hard to believe Tommy is heading towards his old age pension as he still has an almost boyish air of naughtiness and enthusiasm.

Why have The Wurzels been successful for so long? "I don't know, that's the honest truth. I've always believed in enjoying my work and I definitely enjoy this. Maybe that comes across in our music.

"We love playing live. There's nothing like it. The best advice we ever got was in the early days, when a comedian on the same bill asked what we thought we were doing starting our set with a particular song. "We said: 'Oh, that's just a throw away'.

He said: 'If that's how you describe it, then you should do exactly that. You should entertain the audience from the moment you go on stage.' I've never forgotten that advice. We go out there and we give it our all."

The Wurzels have enjoyed a surge in popularity in recent years, expanding their appeal to younger audiences following a performance at Glastonbury Music Festival 2000 and developing a cult following among students.

Their latest album, Never Mind the Bullocks - 'ere's The Wurzels (complete with a cover based upon the famous Sex Pistols album Never Mind the B*llocks), features covers of hits such as Don't Look Back In Anger by Oasis and Rock DJ by Robbie Williams.

Tommy enjoyed a recent appearance with The Cheeky Girls at Brean Leisure Park, but has never forgotten or discarded the gigs that are their bread and butter!

They still play at community centres and weddings – or anywhere else for that matter

"We're appealing to all ages now, which is great," says Tommy.

"People often ask me when we will pack up. I say we'll pack up when we stop enjoying ourselves, and that hasn't happened yet."

Tommy will never forget Adge Cutler, or that tragic day he died in May 1974.

"He crashed into a roundabout near Chepstow," says Tommy.

"He may have fallen asleep at the wheel. I'd seen him pull over in lay-bys to have a sleep before."

The way in which Adge died is one of the reasons why Tommy and his wife Chris and family David & Kate have made their home in Taunton.
He keeps a painting of a beach on his sitting room wall.
"See that," he often tells visitors and friends. "That's a little place called Beer in Devon. We love it there, and not long ago we found a house that would have been perfect.
"But then we thought about the extra driving, and how dangerous that could be coming back late at night from gigs, and we decided it wasn't worth the risk.
"The beauty of living in Taunton is that we're only a few minutes from the motorway."

Two years after Adge's death, The Wurzels hit the big time with a song called Combine Harvester, which was a tongue-in-cheek parody of a song called Brand New Key by a singer called Melanie.
"We recorded it as an album track at the Abbey Road studios and immediately the sound engineer said: 'That's a hit'," recalls Tommy.
"Someone at EMI must have thought the same because it was released as a single. It was the summer of 1976, which was the warmest summer on record until now, and it just took off."
Combine Harvester went to number one in the charts and was soon followed by another hit in I Am a Cider Drinker (played to the tune of Una Paloma Blanca), which reached number three.

Throughout the 1980s and 1990s, The Wurzels were less successful in the charts but they continued to give the barnstorming live performances that had become their trademark.
Their latest album, Never Mind the Bullocks - 'ere's The Wurzels, attracted a cult following after being picked up by Radio 1 DJ Chris Moyles. It includes the track Make Hay Not War – a Wurzelized version of the Catatonia hit Dead From The Waist Down (Make Hay Not War).
Tommy and lead singer Pete Budd re-enacted the famous John and Yoko peace lie-in to express their concern about the war on Iraq.
"We were trying to get across the fact that the Government did not seem to be listening to the feelings of the people of this country."
His own father, Jack, was an army major who was brought up in London's East End and rose through the ranks after joining the Royal Scots.

"He had a wonderful ear for music. He could play the piano, accordion and banjo but it was all by ear," says Tommy.

"The one thing that he always regretted was his lack of education. He'd have loved to have gone to music lessons."

Tommy, the younger of two sons, was to inherit his father's love of music and learned to play piano and accordion.

His work with The Wurzels has given him a particular insight into rural issues. "I saw the way foot and mouth devastated some rural communities," he says.

"It's all very well for these big, managed farms but there are a lot of small farmers who have never really recovered and that kind of thing affects the whole community."

But there plenty of other issues he feels passionate about. "Don't get me started on Europe. We're the only country that actually abides by the EU rules and regulations," declares Tommy.

"I love visiting Spain, and France, and the Greek Islands but when I'm there I'm very much aware that they're in Europe and they don't stick to health and farming regulations in the way that we do.

"But enough of politics, I always try to see the humour in situations. You've got to have a laugh - it's the Wurzel way," he says.

Pete Budd's tales from the Riverbank

"I told my wife that I was going fishing on the River Huntspill – I set off in my blue car, and no-one knew exactly where I would be. I was there enjoying myself on the riverbank, quite a way from the road, when Tommy Banner came rushing up. 'Can you do a gig in Weston tonight?' he asked me. I went home and got ready, and I remember I had to wear Reg Quantrill's clothes – he was twice the size I was, in fact I was pretty skinny in those days. After the gig Adge asked if I would like to join the Wurzels. I played the guitar, but Adge wanted a banjo. 'You can get one o' they and learn to play 'ee,' Adge told me. He didn't realise a guitar had six strings and a banjo just four. But after a week I mastered it, and that was almost 30 years ago!"

Within spitting distance of his old age pension, the second longest serving Wurzel, Pete Budd, is a pretty satisfied fellow. Married to wife Chris for over 40 years, he lives in Devon, has two daughters and seven grandchildren.
A former rock singer, retired Teddy Boy, and self-confessed fishing addict, he has even tried his hand at being a pub landlord in his long and distinguished career.
"I can still remember that day when Tommy came looking for me," he said.
"Reg had decided to leave the Wurzels and Adge was desperate for someone to fill in for the gig in Weston.
"I had known him for ages and also knew most of the songs he was singing. But really my heart was in rock music.
"I had played in various groups, until I formed my own band – Pete Budd and the Rebels. I thought that joining a group like the Wurzels wouldn't be really my scene. It wasn't cool.
"Singing in a rock and roll band at the end of the Fifties and the early 60's was fun. You pulled the girls, and made a few bob pocket money on the side.
"In any case, my dad, who was an engineer, was against me taking a career in music.

"I had been working in the Fry's Chocolate Factory at Keynsham, ordering and dealing with the raw materials, and I believe I would have been in management if I had stayed there.
"When I joined the Wurzels my dad kept saying: 'Why don't you get a proper job? What did you earn last week?'
"Often I had to tell him that my take home pay was nothing! I was waiting for my pay check from the agent.
"He would say: 'That's no good, that won't pay the bills. I told you so.'
"But in fact I was earning about £80 a week in the early days, and that was pretty good money."

The new Wurzel, young Pete Budd, who had a mop of permed hair, was in for a baptism of fire.
"I had a week to learn the banjo and the songs, and then we were off to Germany to entertain the troops," said Pete. "No rehearsals, just straight onto the stage.
"I believe Germany was the place where I learned to drink. I was almost teetotal before I joined the band – but Adge, Tommy and Tony Baylis all liked a drop!
"I remember coming back from one gig after we had drunk a drop, and I felt bad and asked the driver to stop the car, right by a German building site.
"I got out and suddenly some headlights appeared and caught me like a startled rabbit.
"The police appeared, and the tour agent, who spoke perfect German, told them we were an English pop group, and that I had been taken ill.
"They shone the torch on the wheel of the car, and said that they had better get me home or they would arrest me."
Pete said that Adge's motto while he was with the group, was: "Never trust a man who don't drink." Everyone trusted Adge!

During the German tour Adge Cutler and the Wurzels played on the same bill as an orchestra. "The leader asked if the lads could join in some of our numbers. They seemed to like the beat! He asked Adge what key they should play in, and he looked startled and said: "X" will be fine! They must have taken him at his word because we were singing in one key and they were playing in another."

During another foreign tour to Belize to play for the Glorious Glosters, Pete almost got finished off by the sun.

"It was great fun," he said. "We were being flown around by helicopter, staying in bamboo huts, and got taken to a lovely island where the sand was like powder, and the sea was warm and clear.
"But I didn't realise the power of the sun, and got really badly burned feet.
"I received medical treatment in an RAF Hospital every day, and had to be carried by two airmen to get my dressings changed.
"I couldn't get my shoes on and the RSM found me a pair of size 13 training shoes to wear – I normally take sevens!
"I lost most of the skin from my feet, but the show had to go on, and they propped me up so I could play.
"Two years later I met up with the RSM at a music festival. He asked how I was, and then demanded the trainers back!"

The band's fame had spread to the Middle East, and other parts of the world where ex-pats were living.
During one tour, the Wurzels gave a command performance to an Arab Sheik and his family.
"Apparently this very rich bloke's son was studying at Exeter University, heard us play, and went back home and told his dad.
"Our agent laid on a special performance for him, and we played to about 100 people. They were all sat in these huge armchairs in a tiny theatre at his home.
"As we sang, the Sheik's son was stood by his father, whispering in his ear. He was translating the songs – probably telling him what cow dung was!
"Anyway the old Sheik's foot was tapping, and he was enjoying himself – and that's what matters."
During the performance, a keyboard player who had been backing the group, vanished.
"We thought he'd run off," said Pete. "But in fact he had been stumbling around the stage and fallen off the back of it, knocking himself unconscious.
"No one saw it happen – we thought he'd had enough and run off!"

After Adge died in the tragic car crash, Pete Budd and Tommy Banner took the lead in the reformed group.
"We knew it was going to be difficult, but we decided to press on. We tried a couple of new images – like changing the way we dressed – but the public wanted the old Wurzels look, and they accepted our new line-up, without Adge.
"We fulfilled all our existing bookings, and new ones began to roll in. We got some television shows, live gigs and then Combine Harvester went big, and we made the first of 14 appearances on Top of the Pops.

"It was at these shows that we met people like Elton John, and Bob Marley who were also on the same bill.
We also came across Tom Jones on the Ant and Dec Show. He knew our music and was a great bloke. He even invited Tommy to see him in Las Vegas, and go backstage with his family.
"We had a great time on the Ant and Dec Show! Someone had written to Jimmy Saville to sing with us for a Fixit! Ant and Dec got the chap in and he was togged up in a costume like ours, and joined in Combine Harvester."

The Wurzels also met another of their great heroes – World Boxing Champion, Mohammed Ali, at a charity event.
"There were so many nice people out there to help us along," said Pete.
"Paul McCartney met us at the EMI studios when he was recording his Wings Over America album. We were the first to hear the words.
"He did promise to write us a song – but never got around to it.
"But we did write topical songs each week for the Esther Rantzen Show. She is a lovely person too. I remember we wrote one song Worm Charming Day and I had to sing it down the phone to her.
"There was another memorable incident on the Ronnie Corbett Show. He wanted us to appear on quite a lavish set, down some stairs, and then sing The Blackbird Song.
"The music started and as I started down the steps I realised I had completely forgotten the first verse.
"I tried to attract Tommy's attention, but he ignored me. I reached the mike and thank God they just came back to me.
"At that time there was no prompter in front of the cameras. In fact everything we did was live. We were known at the BBC as The One-off Wurzels."

The lads were so good at writing topical songs that they often got calls from television stars and presenters.
"Noel Edmonds rang me up and asked if I could write him a song about Guy Fawkes. Tommy, Tony and I did it, and then he rang me up on Friday night, and said can you do it live on Swap Shop on Saturday night?
"I hadn't even learnt the words so they set up some 'Idiot Boards' with them on. Unfortunately the young girl who should have been turning the cards was talking to a friend. I just gave a big raspberry whenever I forgot the lines.
"Noel hadn't noticed, and told me that probably no-one else had either!
"On another occasion we were playing a Summer Season at the Princess Theatre, Torquay, doing two shows a day with the Bachelors.

"During the break we would go to a little bar down the road for a game of darts.
"One night a customer asked us if we shouldn't be on stage. We legged it to the Theatre where the music had already started.
"Tom was in one wing and I was in the other, and we tried to sneak on and join the dancers without anyone noticing.
"I stepped on one of the dancer's shoes and she limped around the stage, and there was general chaos.
"The audience thought it was part of the show, and roared with laughter.
Tony Baylis, the other Wurzel was not at all amused. He thought it was very unprofessional."

One of the group's favourite acts was Peters and Lee, who they joined in a Seaside Special at the Battle of the Flowers in Jersey.
"Di Lee was a lovely person, and what a voice Lenny Peters had," said Pete.
"Unfortunately Lenny, who was blind, didn't know when people were around him, and often the language would get a bit ripe."
Lenny died, but Di Lee is still on the circuit, and lives in Weston-super-Mare.

"Over the years we have either met or been on the bill with most of the big names," said Pete.
"Our most recent show was Ready, Steady Cook – I was so engrossed with what was going on that I have already forgotten who the chefs were.
"I didn't realise they record three shows at a time, and Ainsley Harriott, who presents it, is a very busy, and very nice bloke."

Pete Budd believes that the Wurzels are lucky to enjoy stardom without the usual pretentiousness that surrounds it.
"I suppose we are of an age where people aren't going to mob us," he said.
"We have a loyal set of fans who follow us around, but when we are not Wurzelling, we easily slip into being civilians again.
"Where I live no-one keeps on about my job. I like a drink down the local where I am just one of the lads.
"I used to run a Devon pub called the Star Inn for seven years, but the Wurzels only played there once.
"I support charities and sometimes we do a local gig, but my mates don't pester me to open things, and all that rubbish.
"I believe I have been very lucky, pursuing my two passions – music and fishing – and making a good living.
"Chris and the other wives sometimes come on gigs with us, and really enjoy it.

"I obviously do a lot of travelling, but the Motorway means that I can get to Tom's house in Taunton, pretty quick, and we travel on together from there.
"The other two lads make their own way – one lives in Swansea and the other in the Forest of Dean, so we are quite scattered.
"We always have an overnight stay if the job is too far from home – we remember what happened to Adge, and learned a lesson from it.
"I do remember that when I had the pub, I often came home in the early hours of the morning, and then had to check the cellar before opening time. It was very tiring."
One problem for the group these days is getting enough of their 'granddad shirts' for the act.
"Cord trousers are easy to get hold of, but the only place where I know they still make and wear the shirts, is Ireland," he said.
"You can imagine that when we take them off they have to go straight into the washing machine. They fade but wear well, and we don't have to change them that often. In fact we hate it when we have to sing in a new shirt."
So what of the future of The Wurzels? Can they become the oldest swingers in town?
"One of my grandsons, 14-year old Kingsley, is interested in music, so he might carry on the family tradition," he said. Although it is unlikely he will ever be a Wurzel.
"Tom and I have discussed the future, and we both agree that when either of us has had enough, then that will be it," he said.
"Until then, we will carry on Wurzelling, and hope people have as much fun as we do."

A young Pete Budd outside his grandmother's house in Brislington, Bristol.

An 18 month old Pete holding a toy train his father made for him.

Pete Budd at Weston-super-Mare's Marine Lake aged about seven on a family day trip. This was his first boat.

Aged about 11 at his grandmother's house in Brislington, Bristol.

Pete in the middle holding the first trout he caught during a holiday at Charmouth. With him are family friends who witnessed his fishing success.

At Rock Fields Studios, Monmouth, recording for EMI in about 1977. Written on the back of the picture is 'woa this cider's working well'.

From left : Alf (brother), Tommy and Alec Cairns (neighbour).

Tommy aged about five, sat on a Second World War garden bomb shelter!

Tommy and big brother Alf.

Tommy with his first accordion.

In Penicuik Park - left to right : Sam Watson, Harry Wright, Sandy Currie, Jake Blaik who is still Tommy's best friend, and Tommy on accordion.

Tommy in Tommy Tulloch's Band, Glencorse Barracks, 1956.

'killer' McFarlane's room 1957. Tommy is second from the left. Tommy says Mr McFarlane was his history teacher. He was known as 'killer' McFarlane because he was 'hard at football'. He was a semi-professional footballer.

East of Scotland Representative side won the Scottish Cup for U-16s. Tommy is front row extreme left.

Tommy, aunt Dolly, mum, dad, brother Alf.

Tommy and Mum.

Jack, Tommy's dad.

Tommy in the early 1960s.

School Sports 1958. Tommy is on the left.

Left to right : Adge Cutler, Tommy Banner, Tony Baylis and Pete Budd at HTV Studio's in Bristol.

Weston Beach. Left to right : Pete Budd, Tommy Banner, Mike Gwilliam (bass player) and in front with the drum John Morgan.

Reg Quantrill, Bryan Walker, John Macey, Adge Cutler, Reg Chant the original Wurzels.

Tommy Banner.

Pete Budd at home with Scrumpy, his Jack Russel.

The Rebels, from left to right: Dave Radford, Pete Budd, Gary Price, John Davis and Ivor Newick.

Left to right : Pete Budd (the one behind with scarf), Tommy Banner (the one behind with hat).

From left to right: Tony Baylis, Tommy Banner and Pete Budd.

Tommy Banner, Terry Pascoe, Pete Budd, John Morgan, Jai Howe performing at BBC studios.

Tommy Banner, Pete Budd and Tony Baylis in the 1970s.

John Morgan on the Forest Beat

"Drink up thy zider? – Not me mate, I prefer a cup of tea. I was lucky to become a Wurzel because Adge didn't like drummers, and especially ones that didn't drink!"

As poor old John Morgan beats out the rhythm for the Wurzels, he knows that the rest of the lads are telling wicked lies about his age.
Old ladies look longingly at the eligible bachelor behind the drum kit, and tell each other: "e's 76 you know – doesn't look it, does he?"
And the reason that John seems younger than the great age that Pete Budd and Tommy Banner have given him, is that he was really born in 1941, and is just 62.
"It's a standing joke in the band – my age," said John, who lives in Aylburton in the Forest of Dean.
"I have no idea how it started, but now people believe that I am on my last legs, and I get pensioner groupies following me around in the supermarket."

The son of a Forest miner, John has enjoyed living in the countryside all of his life. He now shares his home with a Jack Russell terrier called Poppy, a cat and selection of other animals.
"My daughter works in a veterinary surgery, so we get a lot waifs and strays," he said.
After leaving school he became an apprentice electrician until he was 21. But John's great love was music, and played with local groups in the Forest and Gloucester, until he got the chance to turn professional.
"A radio producer for the BBC in Clifton, Bristol – a chap called Brian Patton – wanted a drummer for a group which provided the music that was played to listeners through most of the night.
"We didn't stay up all night, of course, we would go into the studios in the morning and record four sessions a week.
"That was about 30 years ago – time doesn't half fly when you are enjoying yourself.
"I also worked for Mecca for 10 years, and travelled around the Midlands and played in Bath. I also did a lot of gig work for the BBC and played in several Pontins holiday camps.

"I also spent some time at the Dolphin Night Club in Gloucester.
"In fact that was where I first met Adge Cutler and the Wurzels. They were a very big act – top of the bill in fact. I used to love their music, but never thought I would ever play for them.
"It was at the Dolphin that I met some of the real big stars of the 50's. They came to the club and needed a backing group, and I was part of that.
"Vera Lynn, Dickie Valentine and Matt Monroe were some of the people I really enjoyed working with."

As radio changed, so did the type of programmes and music it fostered. The need for light music through the night was coming to an abrupt end. The Disc Jockeys would soon be taking over.
"Brian Patton took me on one side and told me the job with the BBC wasn't going to last much longer," said John.
"But he told me that The Wurzels were looking for a drummer, and that I should apply. It was 22 years ago that I got in touch with their agent, John Miles, and got the job.
"I was over the moon about it. Adge had died eight years earlier, but the band was more famous than it had ever been.
"I was handed a set of corduroys and an old shirt, and suddenly I was a Wurzel."
John enjoys his music so much that he fills in any spare evenings he has got playing with a 60's Rock Band called Bula Bula.
"They come to the Forest now and again, and I love playing the old songs," he said.
"The great thing about being a Wurzel is that none of the lads ever regard what we do as showbiz. It is simply a lot of fun.
"I am being paid for what I enjoy doing, and that's a pretty good position to be in. I have been married twice, but I am a single bloke now, with two lovely daughters.
"I don't go on country walks or fishing, like Pete Budd. I have the countryside all around me to enjoy when I want, but mainly I put my feet up and listen to music, or fiddle around with my computer.
"Of course, everyone around here knows I am a Wurzel, and it does get a bit annoying sometimes when you get stopped in the supermarket.
"I am amazed at the popularity of the band, although most of my own fans are pensioners.
"I agree with the other lads, that when it ceases to be fun, the Wurzels will probably be no more. But in the meantime I will continue to enjoy it.
"Oh! And by the way, this is my chance to tell everybody that both Pete and Tommy are older than me. I am just a toy boy!"

Wurzel Jai had a cracking job before he started singing... cracking safes that is!

You have heard of people going from rags to riches? But in Jai Howe's case it was the complete reverse – he went from being a safe cracker to donning the familiar farmers' wear of The Wurzels.

Perhaps it would be wise to explain at this stage that Jai was never a crook. But he did start out as an apprentice locksmith in his hometown of Torquay, and had a seal of approval for breaking into the safes of local solicitors.

"We would often be called out to crack a safe and recover valuables or documents, and often helped little old ladies who had come out of their homes without bringing the key," he said.

The Wurzels bass player wasn't actually christened Jai! The group's drummer John Morgan gave him the name.

"He didn't want two Johns in the band so he looked for a nickname. He told me I looked like the little boy who lived with Tarzan in the jungle, and his name was Jai. It has stuck with me ever since."

Like the other lads, Jai loves the West Country, and played most of his early music in and around the village halls in his native Devon.

"I had several full time jobs, including working in a Littlewoods Store, but I couldn't wait to get out at nights and weekends and play my guitar," he said.

"I was lucky enough to have my youth in the 1960s, which was a great time for music.

"Our outfit had three guitars and a set of drums, and we used to base our act on groups like the Shadows.

"We kind of changed with the music scene. The Beatles came along, and we sang all their songs. I eventually ended up with a group called The Ventures, who were very well known on the local scene, and we got a lot of bookings.

"I suppose that I became a musician by accident really. I remember being at school during the end of the skiffle era, and there were a couple of my pals messing about with an electric guitar and a snare drum.

"I heard the noise coming from a classroom, and saw an old Tea Chest bass in the corner of the room – you know the sort of thing, it was a wooden box with a broom handle stuck in it, and a piece of string which made a whanging sound when you plucked it!
"A teacher asked me if I would like to have a go, and that's how it all started."

Jai's full-time career was taking a very different course. He worked for a company in Newton Abbot which made artificial knee and hip joints.
"You might laugh, but we also made tiny finger joints, which was very delicate work," he said.
"I remember a poor little girl got crushed in a car accident, and her parents came to us to ask for help, and we produced an entire rib cage for her, made from titanium!
"Unfortunately the company didn't pay very well, and I got myself involved in a strike. Well actually me and another chap didn't want to walk out, but the 2,000 others did, and so off we went.
"The firm was split into two and most of the workforce were involved in making rotor blades for aeroplanes.
"They were being paid six old pence an hour – two and a half new pence – and we asked for a shilling (five pence). The firm offered to meet us halfway, but I left anyway.
"In fact I had met John Morgan who was looking for a full time bass player for his club, The Riverside, in Exeter.
"He was also offering the wonderful sum of £24 a week, which was good money in those days. This was a time when everyone's ambition was to earn £1000 a year!
"It was long hours – starting at 8pm and finishing at 2am, with two, 15 minute breaks."

When John left the Riverside Club Jai went with him to Gloucester, where they met Adge Cutler and the Wurzels for the first time.
"The Witcombe Lodge was an old Polish refugee camp which had been turned into a nightclub, and Adge was often topping the bill," said Jai.
"We went from there to Blackpool, backing cabaret acts, but I got fed up and came back to the West Country, where I teamed up with John's brother, Les Morgan, who had his own group.
"It was called Mavis! And believe it or not, we almost, made it big time. We made a good demo disc and were offered a five-year contract touring the Continent. We were singing soft rock – very tuneful stuff – and I believe we would have gone all the way.

"But I didn't want to leave England, and so we split up. I returned to Devon and teamed up with Terry Pascoe, who had been a member of The Wurzels. We moved to Wales and played in the Rainbow Club, but we could see that the end of live music was in sight.
"The Club Scene was changing, and the age of the disc jockeys had arrived."

Jai met up with his old pal John Morgan again, and sang and played in a Country and Western Band.
"Then Tony Baylis decided to leave the Wurzels and John asked me to come up to Bristol for an audition. This was the mid 1980s when the Wurzels were a five-piece band, eventually discarding the keyboard, and becoming a four-piece group.
"I can recall singing Adge's songs on coach trips, but didn't realise he had written them. I thought they were just West Country folk songs.
"But I became a Wurzel for the first time, left, and then rejoined the lads again in 2002.
"I hope that it is a job that will last me for the rest of my life – I love it. I am 57 now, have a lovely wife Susanne and daughter Kate who is 22.
"I also have a son, Simon, by a previous marriage, who has just told me that I am to become a granddad!
"The great thing about the Wurzels is that fame has never changed the band.
"We have a couple of roadies who do the humping and driving, and we simply have to turn up, get into our costumes, play for an hour and a quarter, and then go home again.
"We can be playing anywhere from a barn to someone's front room – we have a lovely set of fans who follow us everywhere.
"I suppose I am the youngster of the group – we are all getting on a bit now! But I hope to continue Wurzelling for a long while yet!"

Chapter 7

"I wish I was Back on the Farm..."

Wurzels' manager Sil Willcox knew from a very early age that he wasn't going to be an academic. While other pupils at his Bath school were studying for their 'O' and 'A' Levels, he was being picked up by other members of his rock group, and driven to gigs around the country.

"The others would arrive in the exam room, bright-eyed and bushy tailed, while I would have just returned from an all night session, playing clubs and venues around the West Country," he said.

"I was 14, and everyone of that age wanted to be in a group. My parents and teachers told me I would never get a proper job if I continued to miss exams, and they were right in a way. I didn't pass my exams, I was always too late to take them. In any case, all I ever wanted to do was to become part of the music business."

Sil went into printing when he left school. "I was one of a group of people, who would become a rare breed – a hot metal compositor," he said.

"Tears for Fears were very big in those days, and I dreamed of becoming part of a group like that, or even going into management.

"I actually did land a top job in print management. I became sales director, got married, and had a huge salary with company cars for both my wife and myself. What did I do? I gave it all up and went on the dole at the ripe old age of 22.

"I spent the next three years working in bars to get some cash, and to enable me to write songs.

"One of the Stranglers group lived in Box, Wiltshire, and I was invited to join their production crew. We immediately left for the United States, and I have not picked up a guitar from that day to this.

"Since then I have been involved with the Stranglers for 19 years and have been around the world with them, on tour, several times."

Sil remembers telling envious friends that he was part of Rod Stewart's back stage production crew.

"In fact, I was washing up dishes for the great man, backstage, at Wembley Stadium," he said. "I was employed as a member of the catering crew, and took the job so I could see what went on behind the scenes to get a big act on stage. I believe to this day that everyone's job is important. After all, if the dishes aren't washed properly then someone could get food poisoning, and the show would have to be cancelled. I always make a point of saying hello to everyone involved in a show.

"Since those days I have met most of the big names – dined with Paul McCartney and I've also been out with the Rolling Stones.

"I had to find other things to keep the money coming in, and I invented a system to put well know television games inside Christmas crackers. I got the rights to produce versions of the Generation Game, Telly Addicts and Trivia, and sold 72,000 boxes of crackers in one year.

"When I took over the Salamander Pub in Burnham-on-Sea, I was amazed to see boxes of the things stacked near the bar. We turned the pub into a rock venue and the Stranglers played at the opening night."

Sil decided he would try for the big time and become a manager. "The band were going through a lean period and I went to them with a plan. I had never managed a group before and had to meet their accountants and lawyers, but finally they came back and said they would give me a try.

"My first ever gig as their manager took me to Wembley Arena, yards from where I had been Rod Stewart's dish washer, and the band was playing with the Kinks.

"I remember wondering whether or not I had bitten off more than I could chew. It was a steep learning curve, I can tell you."

Sil recalls the early days with the Stranglers, and how they always played The Wurzels music on the coach on the way to gigs.

"I was negotiating with EMI for a contract with the Stranglers, when we were having a meeting in London's Abbey Road Studios, " he said.

"I told the record bosses that I couldn't believe that I was in the same building which had been hallowed by the Fab Four. 'You mean the Beatles?' they asked me. 'No the Wurzels' I told them. They all just collapsed with laughter.

"A while later I knew that EMI was looking for a new manager for The Spice Girls. They sent a message asking me to ring them, and I called thinking they wanted me.

"But they explained that the manager they were looking for was to take over the Wurzels. They remembered my joke, knew I lived on a farm, and said I would be the ideal person.
"So about three years ago I went to Wells to meet the lads – they turned up in a bus with Wurzels written across the front. I think they were playing at a hog roast organised by the local Conservative Club.
"They had no management for about 15 years and were playing for peanuts. I promised them that in future that they would get top billing – their name would appear in larger letters and above the notice for the hog roast!"

The lads did a re-mix of Combine Harvester, and Sil decided the best way to advertise it would be to take a real combine harvester to London, and drive it down Marylebone High Street. Unfortunately the Metropolitan Police had other ideas and threatened to arrest him and the band if the scheme went ahead.
"The press were all there and we had to do something, so we used two miniature combines instead. The record reached 39 in the charts, and the Wurzels donated 50p from each record to the farmers, who were coping with the foot and mouth outbreak at the time."
It was Sil who came up with the idea of getting the Oasis recording of Don't Look Back in Anger, Wurzelised.
"EMI loved the idea and signed up the lads, and they spent a day and a half in my recording studio putting their own brand of humour and style into the single," he said.
"But we were just about to release it when we realised that we had not got clearance from the Gallagher brothers. I called their manager Marcus Russell to negotiate, but EMI were getting worried and refused to release the single until the legalities were sorted out.
"But fortunately Noel Gallagher thought it was brilliant and gave us the go ahead. To publicise the release I got a local farmer to do a corn circle in his wheat field which spelt out the Wurzelised "OO-AR-SIS" and hired a plane from which we could photograph it. It was so successful that we decided to Wurzelise other big names like Robbie Williams and Travis."

Under Sil's management the group's bookings rose to 140 a year, and four recordings have been made at the studio at their manager's home, Charlton Farm near Bath, Somerset.
"Peter Gabriel had created his Real World Studios – mine was on the same lines, but more affordable," said Sil.

The appeal of the countryside has brought top names to Somerset, and they all stay in the farmhouse with Sil and his wife Fiona – taking a trip down to the Tuckers Grave Pub during breaks.
The little pub, which has no bar, and serves beer and cider from barrels in the corner of one of the rooms, has received visits from Mick Jagger, John Moss of Culture Club, and is The Wurzels local.
"I bought the 256 acre farm because of the pub," said Sil. "It is a wonderful place and Tommy Banner and boys love it. Even Glenn Matlock of the Sex Pistols couldn't believe that such a place existed."
The Wurzels and their manager have even attracted the Sunday press pack – in search of a Royal scoop!
"Word got around that Prince William was looking for a special act to appear at his birthday party, and I was asked if I could get an act called Bob Noxious – a really blue and offensive act – to appear with a couple of strippers and some dwarfs! I turned down the offer, but some reporters camped on my doorstep and offered to pay me £20,000 in cash for the story. I declined the offer, but did make them some tea!"

For Sil Willcox, managing the Wurzels is a dream come true. "I have always admired the lads and they give so much pleasure to so many people," he said.

Chapter 8

Wurzelgate

"Listening to Somerset folk singers, sounds like hell," said New Labour's Culture Minister Kim Howells, back in December 2001. "He's talking a load of dung," retorted furious Tommy Banner. This was War – This was Wurzelgate.

The Western Daily Press described it as "The row that rocked the Commons." And Oh Boy! What a furore Culture Minister Kim Howells started when he attacked the music of the West's favourite songsters.
The row - dubbed "Wurzelgate" at Westminster - began in a Parliamentary debate on tough licensing laws which restrict the number of live musicians who can play in pubs.
Liberal Democrat Somerton and Frome MP David Heath argued: "Is it not ridiculous that in the unlikely event of Michael Jackson and Madonna teaming up to do a gig down the local pub they could do so, yet three people singing Somerset folk songs would not be able to do so?"
To which, Mr Howells replied: "For a simple urban boy such as me, the idea of listening to three Somerset folk singers sounds like hell."
Never in the history of politics as a Minister wished so much, that he had kept his mouth shut.

Many of the Commons debates are so boring that even MPs fall asleep. But everyone was wide awake now. The Minister had, probably unwittingly, insulted everyone who rolled their aaaaaaarrrrs!
Tommy Banner hit back, accusing him of "talking a lot of dung", and the Musicians' Union waded in and told him to apologise.
"This guy should get out and about more often. He describes himself as a simple urban boy from Pontypridd - perhaps he should become a more learned rural one," said our Tommy, threatening to wade into the politician with his Wurzel stick.
Ian Smith, organiser of the Musicians' Union's new folk, roots and traditional music section described Mr Howells' remarks as a "bad joke" and called for him to apologise immediately.
"For the minister responsible for culture to make an off the cuff statement like that shows that he does not have the first idea of the wide variety of music we have in the UK," he said.

"This kind of remark makes me very angry and it deserves the kind of reaction it will get."
He said that Somerset folk music had a long and distinguished history stretching back to the beginning of the last century, and was not just about "men in jumpers in the local pub".
Tim Walker, chief executive of the English Folk, Dance and Song Society, said Mr Howells' remarks were "totally outrageous".
"He is talking about the roots of English music. The least we would expect is a formal apology," he said.

In Westminster things were heating up, and Mr Howells was preparing to say sorry. Enter a spokeswoman for the Department of Culture, Media and Sport who refused to say whether Kim Howells would be apologising, but insisted his comments were "throwaway remarks".
Would that be enough to save Mr Howell's face – not a bit of it.
The Western Daily Press carried the story on its front page, and enraged readers jammed the switchboard demanding action.
It was just unfortunate for the Minister that he happened to have an engagement in Bristol – The Wurzels donned their best corduroys and collarless shirts, armed themselves with their instruments, and headed for the city.

Dateline, December 7 – reporter Tristan Cork heads off to ambush Mr Howells with Tommy and the boys, taking a copy of the previous day's WDP, with the headline WURZELGATE emblazoned across it.
Tristan reported: OOOH AAAR! That snooty Culture Minister 'e got a real taste of life in the Westcountry last night, 'e did.
The Wessun Da'y Press teamed up wi' Scrumpy and Western legends the Wurzels to spring a surprise on that there Kim Howells atter 'es swipe at Zomerzet volk music.
Earlier this week he tol' the 'ouse of Commons: "The idea of listening to three Somerset folk singers sounds like hell."
Well, poor old Mr Howells - we certainly raised 'ell for 'im when he turned out ta visit the At-Bristle complex yestday.
The Press arranged for the lads to perform a few of their hits to the Welsh MP to persuade him folk music was as good as his preferred jazz. By the end of a ten minute chat with Wurzels legends Pete Budd and Tommy Banner he was even plugging their new CD.
First, he described yesterday's Western Daily Press "Wurzelgate" front page as "excellent" then he greeted our boys and listened intently.

When the dulcet tones of When the Common Market Comes to Stanton Drew faded away he said: "I really enjoyed that. It was great.

"It is important to say what music you like. My problem is I've always been a jazz fan."

The unlikely enemies parted as good friends after sharing a lengthy conversation which ranged from the merits of Harry Connick Jnr to the particular suburb of Pontypridd, Mr Howells' home town, where Tommy Banner's wife was born.

As event organisers checked their watches it became apparent the Minister and the Wurzels were getting on famously - in fact nobody dared pull them apart.

After the meeting Pete Budd said: "He was a very nice chap. I think he just said a thing on the spur of the moment - we're calling it quits."

The West (The World and Outer Space) is Wurzelised in Song

"Then there were Jenny from Upton Cheney, what a girl were she!
"Girt fat legs, like a couple 'o branches from a chestnut tree."

No one actually knows, or cares, whether there was a real Jenny from Upton Cheney, with robust legs!
There just might have been a Shepton Mallet Matador – who kept rather quiet about his occupation.
The Common Market certainly did come to Stanton Drew – although few people probably noticed, and I suppose the local police chief in North Somerset, could be titled The Sheriff of Midsomer Norton.
But The Wurzels have continued in the tradition of Adge, and ensured that places and characters in his beloved West Country, are remembered in pubs and clubs throughout the area.

Accordionist Tommy Banner freely admits that the favourite songs they perform still go back to the time when Adge Cutler was with them.
The reason behind the success of Wurzel music, is that either an existing catchy tune has been given new words, or the lads have come up with some new music and lyrics to fit it.
Everyone in the audience can also relate to what the lads are singing about.
It would be impossible to examine all their songs in this book – and pretty tedious too – but some of the places and people that have been Wurzelised for eternity, deserve a special mention.
Nailsea has been given a special place, because that's precisely what it deserves. Many of the characters in the early songs would have lived and worked in and around the village.
They were made into caricatures, and then the music was added.
The clever bit was, that the Wurzels then left it to people's imagination, as to whom they were actually singing about.
There was – and still is – many a sly nudge and wink as people relate part of a verse to one of their own pals.

Cutler of the West, which was recorded live at the Webbington Country Club at Loxton near Weston-super-Mare, and featured Adge Cutler, Reg Quantrill, Tommy Banner and Henry Davis, is a classic example of the mixture of original and "borrowed" songs.
Of course the lads led in with Adge's Drink up Thy Zider, but then they launched into a medley of old favourites like MacNamara's Band and I'm Forever Blowing Bubbles.

Then came another of Adge's songs In the Haymaking Time – but it was given a blast of the theme tune from Sing Something Simple, a programme of songs presented by the Adams Singers on Radio Two each Sunday night.
Love or hate the programme, it was instantly recognised, and when you have sunk a pint or two of scrumpy, you enjoy it without even realising!

Some people from outside the area must have left some of the lads' concerts, not understanding a word of what they were singing about.
"Wurzel-speak" – a mixture of the distinctive Bristolian,Somerset, Dorset and Devon dialects, interspersed with Tommy Banner's Scottish tones – often wasn't meant to be understood. Just enjoyed.
Thee's Got'n Where Thee Cassn't Back'n, Hassn't the boys chanted to the delighted Webbington crowd, who joined in with gusto.
But no one actually speaks like that – do they?
The answer is, of course they do. Maybe not as pronounced as the Wurzels, and the dialects are, unfortunately, being consigned to history as people integrate more.
But they are still there.

Before the age of modern transport and communication, making a journey further than 25 miles would have been a major exercise. Any further than 25 miles would have meant an overnight stop.
In those days it would have been almost impossible for any "foreigners" from north of Gloucester, or south of Hereford, to interpret what the people living in the "bit sticking out of the bottom of the British Isles" were saying.
People still measure distances in gunshots, talk about nice things being 'andsome, prefer 'ee told I' to 'he told me.'
I can remember my own grandfather saying: "I'll dap down th' White 'Oss fr a wet 'afor I do go up the wooden 'ill to baid' – which roughly translated, meant that he was going to partake of a pint of beer at the White Horse Hotel before he came home and went upstairs to bed.
Most of us who were born and bred in the area can still roll our aaaarrrrrs!

A concentrated series of elocution lessons, to prepare me for a brief stint on Westward Television, never got rid of my own West Country accent – I am delighted to say.
Comedian Jethro – who has been given a place in my West Country Hall of Fame - is a classic example of someone who has made a fortune from exploiting his dialect.
He has achieved the almost impossible – transported a bit of Cornwall to most countries in the world, and Buckingham Palace!
Another West Country star was Billy Burden from Dorset, who toured the clubs and theatres for three decades, making people laugh by dressing as a yokel, and pretending to be stupid.
Doing the circuit at the same time as Adge, was the late, great, Michael "Shag" Connors and the Carrot Crunchers. He wasn't satisfied with just farmhouse attire, he actually carried a live cockerel around with him.
It delighted the country audiences, but later upset the animal rights campaigners.
The Pigsty Hill Light Orchestra and the Alligator Jug Band were another two acts giving their all, with, what would become to be known as Scrumpy and Western Music.
Even the legendary Russ Conway – also in The West Country Hall of Fame – couldn't resist diverting into some Wurzel tunes when he was playing the Bristol area!

Pill, Pill, I Love Thee Still put another village on the map, along with Sunny Weston Super Mare, Down in Nempnett Thrubwell, The Common Market Comes to Stanton Drew, The Shepton Mallet Matador, The Charlton Mackrell Jug Band, Ferry to Glastonbury, Bridgwater Town, Rock Around the A38 and Mevagissey on a CD called The Wurzels – A Taste of the West.
The recording was made at Charlton Farm Studios, under their new manager Sil Willcox – a far cry from the Number Two Studio at Abbey Road, but none the less very successful.
It features Pete Budd on vocals, banjo and tambourine, Tommy Banner on accordion, piano and vocals, Jai Howe on bass and vocals, and John Morgan on drums and vocals.

The Wurzels spent a day in Shepton Mallet, promoting the town, and their Shepton Mallet Matador track.
As well as being the place where Babycham was invented, Shepton Mallet has been a centre for cider making for as long as anyone can remember.
It doesn't have a matador, or bull ring, as far as anyone knows. But it is the site of Britain's oldest jail, and has the biggest cider mill in Europe!

Just down the road are two other famous sites – the permanent home of the centre of West Country agriculture, The Royal Bath and West Show, and the world's best known farmer, Michael Eavis at Worthy Farm, Pilton.
Farming has been in steep decline for three decades, and the Wurzels have done more than their bit to promote local produce.
They were chosen to create and sing a theme tune for advertising one of the Royal Bath and West Shows.
The lads have also been the guests of the Western Daily Press at two Food and Drink Shows at the showground, and have gone down a storm with the crowds.
Some traders even had to shut up shop for a while when the sounds of I am a Cider Drinker, Morning Glory and I Wish I Were Back on the Farm came bellowing down from the balcony of the Showering Pavilion.
Again, it was probably quite appropriate that they were performing in one of the world's biggest, purpose built, cowsheds, which has also doubled as the venue for a world boxing tournament, pop concerts, antique exhibitions and been graced by Her Majesty The Queen, and many other members of the Royal Family.

At the time of writing The Wurzels are negotiating a second appearance at The Glastonbury Festival or Pilton Pop Festival as Michael Eavis hates it to be known.
I have included Michael in The West Country Hall of Fame, because he has probably done more than anyone to put Somerset on the world map – sometimes for reasons that locals would prefer to forget!
Some of the groups that have appeared on the famous Pyramid Stage at Glastonbury, have already had their work Wurzelised!
Hits from Oasis, Travis, Catatonia, Robbie Williams, Blur and Baby Bird all appear on another of the lads' CDs, appropriate named Never Mind The Bullocks – 'Ere's The Wurzels.
They even released a disc in aid of the Anti-War Movement in March 2003 – Make Hay Not War.

Wurzel fans just might like to know how many places have actually got a mention in their songs over almost 40 years.

Well they include: The A38, Alaska, Arno's Vale, Ashton Gate, Ashton Park, River Avon, Avonmouth, Bangkok, Barcelona, Barrow Gurney, Bath, Bedminster, Birmingham, Blackpool, Blagdon, Blaise Castle, Bombay, Brean Down, Bridgwater, Bristol, Broadmead ,Broom Hill, Burley,Burnham on Sea, Burrington Combe, Calcutta, Cardiff, Catalonia, Charlton Mackrell, Charterhouse, Cheddar, Chesterfield, RiverChew, Chew Magna, Chewton Mendip, Chipping Sodbury, Chittening, Clapton-in-Gordano, Clevedon, Clifton, Congresbury, Costa Brava,Crabapple Hill, Cribb's Causeway, Cumberland Basin.

Denny Island, Devizes, Dings, Dorset, Dover, Downend, The Druids Arms, The Duke, The Dundry, Durdham Down, Easton-in-Gordano, Eastville, Eiffel Tower, Farrington Gurney, The Fawley Feeder, Fishponds Folies Bergeres, Frenchay, Frome.

Glastonbury, Harptree Hill, Hartcliffe, Haslebury Plucknett, Hatch Beauchamp, Henbury, Hinton Blewett, Horfield, Jodrell Bank, John O'Groats, Keynsham, Knowle West, Liverpool, Lockleaze, London, Lulsgate, Malago, Manchester, Mars, Mendips, Mevagissey, Midsomer Norton, Milky Way, Mumbles, Nailsea, Napoli, Nashville, Nelson Street, Nempnett Thrubwell, Norton Malreward, Novers Hill.

Old Market, Paris, Park Street, Pensford, Pill, Pilning, Plymouth, Portbury, Portishead, Priddy ,Radstock, Rose & Crown, Royal Oak, Rudgleigh Inn, St Georges, Saturn, Sea Mills, Severn Beach, Sheephouse Lane, Shepton Mallet, Shirehampton, Singapore, Somerton, Stanton Drew, Stanton Wick, Stogumber, Stogursey, Stratford on Avon, Taunton, Temple Combe, Temple Meads, Timsbury, Tormarton,Totterdown, Treorchy, Ubley, Upton Cheyney, Venus, Webbington ,Wells, West Harptree, Weston Super Mare, The White Lion, Wookey, Yatton and The Zuider Zee.

Chapter 10

The Wurzels' fans and mates!

"Our fan club consists of the loyalist bunch of people you could hope for. We see the same faces many times at our gigs, and that can be a private birthday party with a few people in the room, or at a concert with thousands in the audience. They know all the words to the songs – sometimes better than we do!"
– Pete Budd and Tommy Banner.

They say there's no business like show business, but The Wurzels know that the entertainment world can be fickle. The lads have had good and bad times, but didn't become really famous until after Adge Cutler died.
Unlike most recording artists, they don't carry a huge entourage around with them. Just someone to set up the gear, and load it in and out of their van.
They have changed into their "farmer-style" clothing in "dressing rooms" which range from purpose-built television studio annexes, to gent's toilets, a borrowed bedroom in someone's house, or even behind a screen in a barn.
Costumes aren't a problem either. Most of the lads simply take their shirts and trousers home after a gig, put them in the washing machine, and dry them ready for the next appointment.
"They don't even need ironing," explained Pete Budd. "We all have a favourite shirt, and really don't like it when they have to be replaced."

The fan club is mainly based in the West Country, taking a line from Hereford down to Cornwall. But when West Country folk migrate, either by choice or necessity, then the Wurzels can follow in their wake.
Entertaining an Arab Sheik, as explained in an earlier chapter, or doing a turn for the troops stationed abroad, is all in a year's work.
In the early days The Wurzels recorded their tracks at the famous Abbey Road Studios in London, but now the demand for their CDs is met from a private studio in the heart of the Mendips.
The lads meet with their manager Sil Willcox, who also handles The Stranglers, to re-mix old songs, or experiment with new ones.
Pete and Tommy have been writing songs for ages, and reckon that they can come up with music and lyrics on demand, if a customer or topical story requires it.

One thing is for sure, if any West event has the group billed as part of the entertainment, then the fans arrive in their droves.
The Wurzels took the Royal Bath and West Showground by storm on two occasions in 2003.
At the main agricultural show they were guests of the Western Daily Press in the newspaper's hospitality suite.
They were due to perform near the main ring, but worried organisers felt that Drink Up Thy Zider belting out from the grandstand might just cause the animals to take flight, and stop the crowds concentrating on the main ring events.
They were right too! The Wurzels retreated to an area near the main bandstand and soon the entire area was covered in people, jigging, dancing, singing and simply enjoying the songs.
The fans converged from The Village Green, bars emptied, the shopping mall lost their customers, and the entire Royal Bath and West Show became The Wurzels Show for an hour.
Farmers, children, pensioners and businessmen, couldn't resist letting their hair down, and the cider flowed freely – in fact so freely, that emergency supplies had to be drawn from Matthew Clarks cider mill, just down the road in Shepton Mallet (the place where the Wurzels' legendary Matador was reputed to live).

By popular demand Tommy, Pete and the lads returned for an encore at the showground later in the year – this time for the West Country Food and Drink Fair.
But disaster almost struck! Not the Wurzels, but those of us trying to quench the thirsts of their fans.
Barrels of locally produced Addlestones Cider had been brought from that mill down the road, and several pints had been "tested" by the staff in the Western Daily Press hospitality lounge, set in the veranda above the huge Showering Pavilion, with a birds-eye view of the avenues of stalls and exhibition areas below.
But just as the opening music, heralding the Wurzels' arrival, blared out, the pipes delivering the cider blocked up. This wasn't a pub with no beer – but a congregation of cider drinkers, with no cider.
A very nice man called Simon Russell from that mill up the road again, spent the next hour with a team of helpers, collecting flagons of bottled cider from around the showground hospitality units.
Wurzelling is both thirsty and hungry work, and by the time the first three songs had been delivered by the lads, their fans had eaten up 12 plates of snacks and an entire roasted pig, together with 12 dozen rolls and as many glasses of the cider as four pourers could deliver them.

Afterwards, recovering with a cup of tea at the back of the Show grandstand, Pete confided: "I've never seen the like of it."

Kate Atwell of Clifton, Bristol, wasn't even born when Combine Harvester hit the charts, but she says that the lads not only give her and her friends great pleasure, but actually managed to reunite her dad with lost members of his family: "The Wurzels really are a legend and something us West Country folks should be very proud of.

Being only 23 I am a relatively new fan of theirs, but I have been following them for 10 years now.

The first time I ever remember seeing The Wurzels play live was at the Bristol Community Festival at Ashton Court, when I was a teenager.

When I started seeing my fiancée Chris Kibbey over seven years ago, I found out that he was a fan too. We both watched them play at Finnegan's Wake Pub in Cotham (now The Cotham Hill). But since then we have been to many of their gigs, including the Glastonbury Festival.

In summer 2002 my dad saw an advert for a charity Wurzels show at a farm in Claverham. When he enquired about tickets he found that the farm was run by members of the Atwell family!

That particular event was one of my favourites, in a barn in the middle of summer. We dressed up, Wurzel-style, and had our photos published in the Western Daily Press."

Frank Huddy from Chard, Somerset, actually backed the lads when dear old Adge Cutler was alive.

"I booked Adge Cutler and the Wurzels several times and played opposite them as a band leader at various venues in the West.

My band – the Tony Graham Combo – travelled the South and West of England for 23 years, and recall the master Wurzel showman, Adge, who was a very talented songwriter and a true gentleman on the stage.

"One of my best memories was when I booked them at Axminster, and did the support with my own band. To see Adge in full flow, Wurzel stick in frantic action and cavorting across the stage was a never to be forgotten sight.

Their fee at that time was £100 – and they were worth much more.

Bridget Smith from Ilminster, Somerset, saw the Wurzels posing for a picture for one of their record labels, and managed to get it autographed.

"The picture was taken when I was still at school, and I am 53 years old now. I put in on my bedroom wall, and when I got married, 22 years ago, I took the photo with me, and it still has pride of place in our house."

David and Greta Thrush from Carhampton near Minehead recall the days when The Wurzels arrived to help their local pub, The Butchers Arms, wassail the local apple tree.

"We had a huge bonfire in the pub orchard, and glasses of spiced cider were passed around. Wassailing ensures a good crop the following year, and involves putting a piece of toast, soaked with cider, into the branches of the tree to feed the good spirits (The Robins).
Gunshots are then fired to scare away the evil spirits, and we all joined in the Wassail Song with the Wurzels.

Old Apple Tree we Wassail thee
And hope that thee will bear
'Ats full, Caps full and dree (three) bushel bags full
And a little heap under the stairs
Hip, Hip, Hooray!

We remember that Tommy Banner was there, and also the Yakima Wassail Queen from Yakima State, USA, who brought us a special cup and a gift of red apples.
After Adge's death we were so glad that the Wurzels decided to keep going. Goodluck to them, and long may they continue to bring laughter and fun to so many."

Bob Gibbons from Dinder near Wells, is still trying to get his own back on Wurzel Pete Budd, after a prank he played on his wife more than 50 years ago.
"My wife and I were at junior school together, and Pete Budd was in our class at Wick Road, Brislington in the late 1940s and early 50s.
I remember we had a good football team, but one Saturday morning we were short of our regular goalkeeper, and we were due to play in South Street, in what was expected to be a close encounter.
Pete Budd volunteered to go into goal, and we lost 10 – 0! He was never asked again.
And my wife, formerly Jill Rockett, recalls that Pete chased her home from Jubilee Swimming Baths one day, threatening her with a matchbox in which he kept his pet grass-snake!"

Mike and Jean Frecknall from Shepton Mallet have an even saucier tale, about the night they saw a naked Wurzel on a caravan roof next door to where they were staying.
"It was summer 1974 and we were holidaying in our caravan at Croyde Bay in Devon.

In the camp club, an up and coming group called The Wurzels were the main act. They were also staying in the next caravan to ours.
One night there was quite a commotion outside and when my wife looked out she saw, through the darkness, a figure on top of the caravan roof, attempting to get in through the skylight.
The odd thing was that the fellow was stark naked.
A couple of years ago we met up with the Wurzels at the Mid Somerset Show in Shepton Mallet, and my wife related the story to Tommy Banner, who admitted he was the one on the roof minus his clothes.
He had been kicked out by the others in the caravan for making too much noise. They locked the door and so Tommy, in all his glory, climbed onto the caravan roof to try to get back in. He was astonished that anyone would remember the incident after 30 years.
We became fans at Croyde Bay and we have some lovely memories of the lads, who have brought much joy to millions of people."

Ivy and Bill Abbott of Redlynch, Salisbury, will put anyone right who thinks that the lads might be tight with their money!
They asked for an autograph back in the 70s, and received a £1 note signed by four members of the band.

David Williams from Woolavington near Bridgwater, managed to dress up in an even older, and more outrageous, costume than the lads themselves, when he met them in September 1968 at the local Albion Rugby Club's Tramps' Ball.
"I attended the event in an old Army greatcoat, old pair of jeans, one boot and one shoe, and didn't shave for two days before the night.
I covered my face with mud and prepared a snack of sausages, which I carried in a polythene bag in a dirty old tin, tied into a knapsack on the end of a pole.
I won the prize for the Champion Tramp and was called up on the stage by Adge and the lads. There was Reg Quantrill, Henry Davis and Tommy Banner supporting Adge. We filled the cup with zider and joined in a toast – I managed to look scruffier than they were."

Extra Wurzels

Ready, Steady Cook

Television has brought the Wurzels into the living rooms of millions of people up and down the country, either in adverts, guesting on shows, or even trying their hands at cooking.

Both Pete and Tommy normally leave the cooking to their respective wives, but couldn't resist a challenge to help produce eight meals in just 20 minutes, on the BBC 2's Ready Steady Cook programme.
Celebrity chefs Phil Vickery and Tony Tobin were the unsuspecting teachers, with Ainsley Harriott trying to keep control of the proceedings.
But viewers did get another insight into the skills of the lads – both Tommy and Pete revealed that they actually do cook at home, and have to do the washing up.
Millions of viewers also heard from Tommy how they got to play at Buckingham Palace – by Royal Appointment.
"We were invited by the great Anne Shelton," said Tommy. "But during our act the sound went down, and when we came off stage we had a go at the sound engineer. But he told us that a message had come down from one of the Royals to turn the noise down – not the music, but the noise."

Tommy was very hands on in the BBC kitchen, and managed to cook a selection of pea pancakes and insisted on being given a full range of jobs to do by Phil Vickery.
Pete did sing "I am a Zider drinker," but was less energetic, admitting that his two daughters tend to think he is interfering if he tries his culinary skills at home.
But the lads did manage to produce some pretty tasty food in their 20 minutes.
Tommy ended up with "Wurzel Grubbage" – rib-eye steak stuffed with Stilton cheese and onions, with chips, and sweet and sour sauce.
Pete, who confined his cooking to melting a stock cube into water, had grilled steak with chips, pea soup, pea dipping sauce and skewered beef, then double cream and egg yolks soufflé.
The audience decided (on a close vote) that Tommy and Phil won the day, and declared the day to be brilliant.

Left to right : John Morgan, Tommy Banner, Leslie Nielson of Airplane and Naked Gun fame, Pete Budd.

Left to right : Pete Budd, Tommy Banner, John Morgan and Dave Wintour.

Tommy Banner and Pete Budd with two members of Chaos UK.

Left to right: Tommy Banner, Dave Wintour, John Morgan, Pete Budd at Netley Marsh Steam Fair.

Pete Budd and Tommy Banner opening "Cousin Jacks" Pasty Shop in Bristol.

Bristol City v Port Vale...the Wurzels entertain at half-time as part of the Centenary Celebrations.

The Wurzels perform at Bristol's Broadmead.

Drink up Thee Zider - the Wurzels appearing at Swindon Apple Day in 2001.

Pete and Tommy enjoy some cider with Dave Wintour and John Morgan.

The Wurzels read all about the Wurzelgate scandal rocking Westminister while waiting to confront Minister Kim Howells as he visits @Bristol, 6th December 2001. The front bencher had been slammed for describing listening to the Wurzels as 'sounding like hell'.

Pete Budd, John Morgan, Tommy Banner and Mike Gwilliam outside The Black Horse at Clapton in Gordano.

Tommy and Chris.

Pete Budd and Tommy Banner at Ascot Ladies Day.

Chris's Mum Ethel,
Kate, Chris, Tommy.

The Wurzels at the Royal Bath and West Show in Shepton Mallet on June 2 2004.

Pete Budd and Tommy Banner.

Fans appreciate the Wurzel's at the Bath and West Show, 2004.

Pete and Tommy performing at the 2004 Bath and West Show.

John Morgan.

(Above & Left) Wurzels at the Royal Bath and West Show 2004.

Alexander, Lord Bath surrounded by the Wurzels, Tommy Banner, Pete Budd and Jai at the Western Daily Press Suite in the Royal Bath and West Showground.

Western Daily Press competition winners meet The Wurzels before the City v QPR match on April 3 2004.

Louie Nicastro who co-produced with George Allen "Never Mind the Bullock" and who sole produced the albums "Live over Mendip" and "Taste of the West".

Somerset music legends The Wurzels manager Sil Willcox, Tuesday 11 May 2004, in the recording studio at his farm near Bath, Somerset.

West Country Hall of Fame

Mr Acker Bilk

Bernard Stanley Bilk (Acker being Somerset dialect for 'mate') may be a jazz legend, but he has always had his feet firmly on the ground. He is proud to play in his local town of Pensford, and loves the West Country.

Acker is the chart-topper who hated London and was not afraid to admit it and leave the big city. He will still go anywhere the music takes him, he's still experimenting, still improvising, still keen to collaborate with other musicians.

But there is something in the woods and fields, perhaps even the air, of the old Somerset mining village that feeds his soul. And maybe that is what has fed his God-given talent to make music that can range from hugely joyful to hauntingly melancholic.

It's natural enough that a country boy who was able to run wild with his mates, poach the odd rabbit and toboggan down the coal tip should remember his childhood with affection.

It was a world away from the beer bar in post-war Dusseldorf where Acker and his Bristol Paramount Jazz Band got their big break, or the jet-set world he enjoyed in the 1960s following his UK-US chart-topper, Stranger On The Shore.

When he was a lad, Acker's parents tried to teach him the piano but he resented being kept away from the countryside.

When he lost half a finger in a sledging accident, music making must have seemed even farther away, but now he reckons that missing half-digit is responsible for his distinctive style of playing.

The son of a cabinet-maker, Acker left school at the age of 14 and took a job at Wills' tobacco factory in Bedminster. The only alternative was farm labouring or going down the pit and he was the envy of many, but the idea of doing the same job in the same place for the rest of his life did not appeal to the free-spirited teenager.
He stuck it for three years until National Service carried him off to the Suez Canal Zone, and an encounter that was to change his life.

To relieve the boredom while off duty, Acker borrowed a military clarinet and began to play, copying whatever records came his way. Sent to the glasshouse for sleeping on duty he endured the boredom by practising the instrument.

When he was demobbed he came back to the West and formed his first band, in Bristol. Then he and wife, Jean, his childhood sweetheart, moved to London so Acker could join the Ken Colyer Band. But he hated London and returned to Bristol to form the Bristol Paramount Jazz Band.

In 1951, the band went to London and Acker and Jean lived in a factory attic in Plaistow until the band got its first big break - six weeks constant playing in a beer bar in Dusseldorf. That really disciplined the band and it never looked back.

Hit records followed and then in 1961 Acker recorded Stranger On The Shore, the first-ever recording to be number one simultaneously in the UK and USA. It was 55 weeks in the charts and last year - its golden jubilee - was acclaimed as number 58 in the all-time hits league.

In his seventies Acker still has a very busy international Programme like jetting off to Hungary to take part in a Dixieland Festival.

He is constantly asked to guest with other bands but says his loyalties lie with the Paramount. He accepts an occasional solo gig in Bristol and meets up with Humphrey Lyttelton, Chris Barber or Kenny Ball and his Jazzmen. He also appeared with George Melly in Giants of Jazz.
Home for many years has been a bungalow in Pensford, overlooking his beloved Somerset countryside.

These days he is as likely to be seen with a paintbrush in his hand as a clarinet.

He began oil painting several years ago and though he is modest about his ability, he loves capturing the landscape around Pensford in Impressionistic style.

He is not alone. He says: "Four of us, all ex-Paramount Jazz band men, go out to paint every week. There is Dave Collett, Jay Hawkins who used to play banjo, Roy Smith an ex-drummer and Q Williams, who was piano.

Music will always be my first love but we really enjoy our painting."

Painting helped Acker through a tough six months from October 1999 to April 2000 when he was being treated for throat cancer. Willpower and first-class medical treatment got him through that time.

Russ Conway

Russ Conway was the honky-tonk pianist with the glittering smile who entertained generations of music lovers without ever forgetting his roots.
He coped with ill health, near bankruptcy and a drink problem to remain at the top of his profession far longer than most of his contemporaries.
The Queen Mother's favourite rose from humble beginnings in Bedminster, Bristol, to rub shoulders with the worlds finest entertainers.

He had 17 consecutive chart hits that sold more than 30 million records in the late Fifties and early Sixties – before the Beatles were even on the scene.
But he never forgot his childhood home and friends remembered how he had asked for his ashes to be scattered in the city.

Many Bristolians remembered him best for his triumphant return to the city in 1995 when he raised thousands of pounds for his cancer charity by performing at the Hippodrome. He thought he had beaten the cancer which eventually took his life and wanted to do something to help other people suffering from the disease.

Russ Conway - whose real name was Trevor Stanford - was born on September 1, 1925. He had no formal musical tuition except for one piano lesson at the age of four.

At the age of ten he won a scholarship which enabled him to gain entrance into the choir of a church school in Bristol.

He left school aged 14 and his father - a commercial traveler - placed him in a solicitors' office. However, he was sent to borstal for three years for the theft of money which he found in a packet. Although he still found a piano to play.

But he wanted to go to sea and finally, after his release, his father allowed him to enter a Merchant Navy Training School. At the end of his third trip he was rushed to hospital with appendicitis.That, however, did not deter him. In 1942, he joined the Royal Navy.
He took part in mine-sweeping operations in the Aegean and the Mediterranean, and was awarded the DSM for "gallantry and devotion to duty" during these operations.
After being demobbed, Conway found it difficult to adapt to civilian life and he rejoined the Merchant Navy, only to be discharged in 1948 with a stomach complaint.

For four years, he worked as a salesman, machinist, plumber's mate and barman.

He rejoined the Merchant Navy yet again, but after three years his stomach illness returned.

It was after that while doing a pianist stint at a club that he was "discovered" by one of England's top choreographers, Irving Davies.
He was soon accompanying the likes of Lita Rosa, Denis Lotis, Dorothy Squires, Shani Wallis, Adelaide Hall and even the great Gracie Fields. He was known variously as the Prince Charming of Pop and the King of the Keyboard.

Later he worked with Sir Laurence Olivier and John Mills, helping to perfect the routines and orchestration's for their memorable performances in the "Night of 100 Stars" at the London Palladium.

He also wrote additional music for the Circus Ballet in the English production of the American musical Fanny. He became a TV favourite on variety shows, working regularly with Billy Cotton for a time. He was the first performer to win a silver disc, when his hit record Roulette topped the 250,000 sales mark, a total which was rapidly equalled by three other of his hits, Sidesaddle, China Tea and Snow Coach. He starred in a string of Royal Command Performances and remained Queen Elizabeth the Queen Mother's favourite pianist for more than half-a century.

But illness and injury continued to dog him. He lost part of a finger in an accident, chipped a hip bone in a fall – which paralysed him for three days - and he collapsed over the keyboard at a Scarborough show. This was followed by a nervous breakdown. In December 1965, Conway suffered a mild stroke and was ordered to rest. But he recovered and made a comeback in the TV Palladium Show several months later.

In 1971, he was, to use his own words, becoming difficult to work with. He had started drinking at a pace which reduced him from considerable wealth to near bankruptcy. But his friends helped to pull him through.

Conway's career resumed, but on a much smaller scale. He toured the provincial theatres, usually packing them out with his by now mature fans. But in 1990, he discovered that he had cancer in his stomach, which after months of intensive treatment, he appeared to overcome. He set up the Russ Conway Cancer Fund, producing annual shows to raise money for cancer-related charities.

Once he was asked what made him smile on stage, and he replied: "Oh, I think of somone who doesn't like me, and then I think of my bank balance." Conway did not marry.

Alfred Hawthorn (Benny) Hill

Adge Cutler admired another son of the West, one Alfred Hawthorn Hill - better known to millions of television viewers around the world, as Benny Hill.

Many of the comedian's characters were of the same, rustic nature as those portrayed by Adge, who actually did his own version of a Hill hit, called Harvest of Love.

The song told the story of a love-smitten farmer, who related in verse, and not very complimentary method, his bid to woo a young lady.

As I plough the field nearby
Your memory I can't erase!
For as a I walk to the rear of the horse my dear,
I seem to see your face!

Benny Hill was born in Southampton in the south of England in January 1925, into a family which would have fitted into the lower middle class category.

His father was the manager of a medical appliance company, and for family treats would take them all to the two variety theatres in the town, where young Alfie became entranced by the actors and their characters.

In the later years of World War Two he was called up for his National Service, and found that he was better at entertaining his mates in the Royal Engineers, rather than fighting the enemy.

He shunned the idea of following in his father's footsteps, and when he was demobbed he applied for, and got, bit parts in variety theatres, as a comedian.

He had an uncanny knack of watching and imitating people, and would sit quietly for hours, just making notes of characters who passed by.

His big chance came in 1956, when the Ealing Studio sent out an SOS for comics to appear in a feature film Who Done It? , and Mr Hill got the part of a hapless, bungling, private detective.

By this time he had already changed his name to Benny - after his comic hero, Jack Benny.

Audiences would watch almost anything after the War years, and cinemas were popular in the 1950s. But the Ealing film was only mildly funny and did not shoot any of the actors into stardom.

But a new medium - television - was being rapidly developed, and Benny Hill saw his chance to reach millions of people.

To begin with, Tony Hancock, took the limelight, but after his untimely death, Benny Hill began to shine through, with his routine of comic songs and sketches - from the very figures such as Tony Hancock and later performers such as Frankie Howerd. Whereas Hancock established his definitive comic persona in radio and then extended this to television, Hill was in effect created by television. Yet Hill was also the most traditional of comedians and his programs had strong roots in variety theatre, revolving around comic songs, routines and sketches rather than an on-going comic characterisation and situation. And although beginning, rather risqué in places.

In 1955 the BBC decided to launch a series of variety shows, to be fronted by individual comics.

Ken Dodd, Charlie Drake and Frankie Howerd were signed up, along with Benny Hill.

Part of Benny's genius lay in his writing. He wrote all his own material, a gruelling task which explains the relatively small number of programs produced.

Thames Television signed him up, but the Benny Hill Show was not scheduled far ahead in time. The television bosses had to wait until Benny had been out and collected enough material for his sketches and songs, and then it would be made. into offshoots of The Benny Hill Show such as the 1970 half-hour silent film Eddie in August.
The shows were broadcast to huge audiences, who couldn't get enough of the original Cheeky Chappie!

Much of the content was the type of humour found on seaside postcards, but Benny Hill's love of travel also introduced international characters, like the immortal Chinese businessman, Chow Mein.

He got away with material, which would now be regarded as politically incorrect, simply by playing on different languages and dialects - uttering something which was completely rude, and then quickly introducing an explanation that it had been merely misinterpreted, and had a completely different meaning.

All his Japanese characters had large teeth, Germans were arrogant, West Country people were pretty unintelligent - all, including his dim-witted Fred Scuttle were hilariously funny.

Although all his material was original, Benny nevertheless owed a comic debt to U.S. entertainer, Red Skelton. Like Skelton, he worked in broad strokes and sometimes in pantomime with a series of recurring comic personae. Benny even adopted Skelton's departing line from the latter's show that ran on network television from 1951 to 1971: "Good night, God bless."

The seaside, postcard humour, of henpecked and shrunken older men and randy young men, both attracted to beautiful young women with large breasts and frequently tearing or missing some of their underwear, was Benny's trademark material. The shows always ended with a chase, taking people back to the days of the Brian Rix farces.
His most famous record - Ernie, The Fastest Milkman in the West - was a comic documentary of his early life in Eastleigh, Hampshire, where he actually worked as a milkman, delivering to one of the biggest housing estates.

Far from being the fastest in the West he was sacked for being too slow! He would stop and talk to the pretty young women on his round. Many of the characters he met, and the streets he visited are immortalised in the song.

While Benny was often portrayed him as a kind of playboy who liked to surround himself with beautiful, leggy showgirls, in fact he was a lonely and solitary figure. He never married, and lived alone in what would have been a depressing existence, had it not been for the heavy work demands imposed by the television show.

His humour with its smut and double-entendres was never entirely acceptable to the moral standards of some and his sexism made him seem increasingly old-fashioned.

The forces of political correctness finally had their way in 1989 when Thames Television cancelled the programme, due not to only complaints about its smuttiness but also because its old-fashioned sexism had become increasingly intolerable.

Thames finally sacked Benny. It was a blow to both his pride and lifestyle. He could never understand why a company, for which he had done so much, should treat him so badly. In his last television appearance, in 1991 he appeared as himself, the subject of the BBC arts documentary series, Omnibus.

Although over the last three years of his life, Benny was to talk in interviews about a comeback, it was the end of his career.

He died alone in his flat, surrounded by this three television sets, and sparse furniture in 1992. More drama was to follow, when his grave in Southampton cemetery was attacked - police believe that someone tried to dig up his body, while searching for money which was rumoured to have accompanied him to his grave.

Benny Hill once told an interviewer that, like Van Gogh, he would be appreciated in 100 years time. The statement implied that he was not recognised as a great comedian and was belied by the enormous international popularity of his program and by the fact that in the 1970s and 1980s he was several times voted the Funniest Man in the World by the British television audience.

Since his death The Benny Hill Show has been broadcast around the world - he is still being seen, and enjoyed, at least once a day.

Jethro

The art of taking the West Country dialect around the country - and still being understood - has been mastered by one of Britain's best ever stand-up comics Geoff Rowe.

In the 70's he was booked as support act for The Wurzels and in later years they would support him.

The fact that he looks like a farmer's son is not surprising - for the man we all know and love as Jethro, was born on a farm in 1948, in the Cornish village of St Buryan.

He didn't have to work on his Cornish dialect either - working as a local carpenter, and then as a timber man in a tin mine, meant he was always rubbing shoulders with men who had that distinctive West Country burr!

He used his wonderful bass voice to entertain customers in local pubs - and also cracked jokes, based on local places and characters.

Within a few months of his first performance, he established himself as Cornwall's top comic, and people came from miles, packing pubs ands clubs, to hear him.

The soft, Cornish voice, with a slight lisp, coupled with Jethro's tremendous sense of humour, has left members of the Royal Family in tears of laughter.

At the age of 18 he took to the stage, first in the chorus, and then taking a principal part with the St Just and District Operatic Society.

People were more enhanced with his jokes than his singing - although he did have a very good voice - and both he, and they, realised that he had a very special talent for making people laugh.
Since those early days he now sells over a quarter million theatre seats a year, appearing in over 170 theatres and has an enormous cult following.
His theatre tour takes him all over the country including Aberdeen, Carlisle, Chesterfield, Norwich, Oxford and Southampton, plus many more.

Over the years Jethro has made a record nine appearances on Des O'Connor Show (he first appeared on Des O'Connor Tonight in 1990 and in the same year on Des O'Connor Christmas Eve Show, the first time any comedian had been invited back on the same series). He has appeared on Jim Davidson's Generation Game five times, twice to make a Cornish Pasty! In fact, Jim is a big fan of the Cornish Comic and says Jethro is his favourite storyteller. He also hosted two shows of his own for H.T.V. "The Jethro Junction" which were a great success. However, in December 2001 Jethro was particularly honoured to appear in the Royal Variety show in front of the Queen.
Jethro lives in Lewdown on the Devon/Cornwall border. His great love is his horses, which he shows all over the country and has won most major prizes including Wembley. Two other sporting loves are golf, his club is St. Enedoc in Cornwall and Rugby, he played for Penzance and Newlyn Senior First Team for 10 years 1967 to 1977 as prop forward. One of Jethro's team-mates at the time was Stack Stevens who went on to become one of English Rugby's most famous players.

In March 1995 Jethro walked from Lands End to Lewdown (approx. 100 miles) to raise money for the Bristol Cancer Open Scanner Appeal. He performed a show each night at various venues along the way and raised £20,000. A pasty drop by helicopter en route helped to keep him going! In August 1996 Jethro's Irish Cajun at his club raised a further £4,000 for the appeal with more funds being raised at this very successful event in 1997 and again in 1998.

In 1993 Jethro released his first video "A Portion of Jethro" which sold nearly 150,000 copies, outselling everything else in some parts of the country, including Jungle Book.

Unsurprisingly he is managed by the man who discovered Adge Cutler - Mr John Miles.

"I speak to him most nights when he is travelling back from a gig," said John. "He is so naturally funny that even when he is being serious, I wonder if there is a joke on the way."

The Yetties

No tribute to Adge Cutler and the Wurzels would be complete without a mention of another famous West Country group - The Yetties, who hail from Yetminster in Dorset, and to where they regularly return to give concerts. Songs, stories and comedy from the West of England have gained the group a massive following around the world, over the past 37 years. They turned professional in 1967, just after Adge founded his group, and had the same beginning- singing in local pubs and clubs, before being recognised as having a remarkable talent.

Their music and their enthusiasm has taken them far beyond the villages of Dorset. They have travelled extensively in Europe and, under the auspices of the British Council, have performed successfully in many countries, including Thailand, Nepal, Sri-Lanka, Malaysia, Hong Kong, Singapore, Pakistan, Sudan, India, Bangladesh, The Maldives, The Philippines, Ethiopia and Canada. They have the knack of breaking down language barriers and getting people involved in what they do. Audience participation in a Yetties show is a very important ingredient and people do join in from the word go whether they are 9 or 90.

Over the years they have recorded no less than 45 albums for different companies. Most of these have been a mixture of songs and music but they have also been involved in some other fascinating projects.

Thomas Hardy (the Dorset writer and poet) was also a musician. He and his family, over several generations, collected hundreds of folk tunes. The Yetties have done two recordings using Thomas Hardy's own fiddle and other Hardy family instruments.

So, because of The Yetties, Hardy's violin was brought back to life and so were his favourite jigs, polkas, reels and waltzes. Another recording of which they are extremely proud is a collection of songs and stories about cricketers of the past with John Arlott.

The Yetties have never lost their genuine feeling for the countryside. They now live in Sherborne (just a few miles from Yetminster) and they draw on their personal experiences of country life for their concert programme. Some of the songs they sing recall what life was like when they were kids helping the farmers at harvest time, scrumping when the farmers weren't looking, raiding the hedges, fields and woods for food and eating rabbit for practically every meal. They talk of village characters and village occasions and create the atmosphere of the village social.

The Yetties represent the heart and soul of England, which is still there if you dig deep enough. Modern technology has changed our life styles a tremendous amount but people don't change that rapidly they still, given the chance, like a good old sing-along of a Saturday night.
Adge Cutler wrote his most famous songs for The Wurzels when he was growing up in Nailsea near Bristol. But as archiver Gerry Brooke discovered, it's not "Drinking up Thy Zider" that it is remembered for.

It may not seem much like an industrial centre these days but the large North Somerset village of Nailsea was once the site of a big business enterprise.

No, not the scrumpy and Western music business started by the late Adge Cutler of Wurzel fame or even the much-lamented Coates cider factory, but a glassworks.

For Nailsea lies at the centre of a small coalfield which has been worked since late medieval times. It once supplied fuel for the Smyth family of Ashton Court, who owned the pits. It was this source of coal, plus plentiful lime, stone, sand and clay that attracted a Bristol cooper and glassmaker, John Lucas, to the area in 1788.

He sold his beer and cider works, borrowed £4,000 (an enormous sum in those days), leased six acres of land and constructed two 80 foot high brick cones, one for making window glass and one for making bottles.
As there were no skilled glass workers in the area, Lucas was forced to import whole families from other glass works all over the country. In 1792 when the social reformer and bluestocking Hannah More visited the works from her home in Wrington, there were about 200 (employees) on the site living in a whole row of newly-built cottages.

There were eventually 34 homes, all built by Lucas for his workers and families. Labour was mostly highly skilled, but very hot and arduous, and the whole fusion process took anything from 18 to 30 hours non-stop. But it was highly paid, with top employees (gaffers) earning double or triple the average manual wages of the day.

They lived well, having meat and vegetables every day. They even ate snails, a great delicacy in those times.

Bottles were only manufactured for the first 40 years, from then on the works made only window glass, which was melted and then cut on large tables 50 inches in diameter. It was known as Crown glass, and had a pale greenish tinge to it and a bulls eye in the middle. It is remembered in a Nailsea place name today.
Later, as techniques improved, sheet and then plate glass was produced. Lucas became rich, building himself and family a mansion - Backwell Hill House - on the site of an old hunting lodge. By early Victorian times Nailsea was the fourth largest producer of glass in the country, exporting to Ireland, West Indies and the Americas.

Transport was always a problem, with the glass having to be carefully packed in straw and then taken by wagon (a dilley) and turnpike road on the ten-mile journey to Bristol's Temple Meads railway station, or the ships in the city docks.

This was expensive and plans were made for a canal from Morgan's Pill on the Avon up to the site, but these eventually came to nothing, and up to 10,000 crates of glass a year continued to go to Bristol by cart.
Despite this vast output, most of the so-called Nailsea Glass -so desirable today - was not actually made in the village at all!

What was made were so-called friggers - bits and pieces made by workers from spare glass left over at the end of a shift. Using all their skills, such items as barley sugar walking sticks, rolling pins, door stops, paperweights and the like were produced and sold locally.

In later Victorian times things started to go wrong for the company. The coal supply failed and glass production moved to Birmingham and the north.

Despite careful ownership closure came in 1873. In 1905 a brick cone was blown up and later used as hard core for the massive Brabazon runway at Filton.

Later other cones were felled and the site became derelict and overgrown, with only a few buildings and workers' houses left standing.

Excavations in the 1980s revealed many lost secrets and now new excavations for a Tesco store have revealed yet another unknown coal pit.

It is believed to have been part of the Glasshouse Pit, which produced fuel for the town glassworks. Local historians have already listed 27 pits and more than 100 mine shafts in the area.

Nailsea desperately needs a museum to display this heritage but until then small collections of Nailsea glass can be seen at both Weston and Bristol museums as well as at Clevedon Court, which is open during the summer months.

Drink Up Thy Zider...A note on the Wurzels most famous tipple!

A passion for cider has existed for centuries. In 1708, J. Philips, the English poet, wrote an epic style poem, (spanning two volumes!), called "Cyder". He elevates cider to glorious heights and enthuses that only the best apples should be used,
"...thy Press with purest Juice
Shall flow...".

What is cider?

Most cider is made from fermented apple juice. Natural cider has nothing added and relies, for fermentation, upon the wild yeast present in the apples. For mass-produced ciders, a yeast culture is added in order to achieve consistency.

Although much of today's cider is produced from apple concentrate, many traditional cider-makers use only cider apples, cultivated specifically for the purpose.

Both traditional and mass-market ciders are available carbonated or still and range in style from the bone dry, to the extremely sweet. In Europe, "cider" refers to (fermented) apple juice that contains varying levels of alcohol.

In the USA, fermented apple juice is known as "hard cider"; unfermented, freshly expressed juice is called "sweet cider."

A thirst for decent, real cider has led to much experimentation amongst world cider producers.

New, flavoursome cider apples are constantly being developed to meet popular demand.

Nowadays, modern varieties called Kingston Black, Brown's Apple and Yarlington are being planted alongside traditional cider apples such as Foxwhelp, Blood Butcher and Slack-my-Girdle.

A fresh optimism is sweeping through the cider industry. Today's cider producers are bubbling with confidence.

Cider has never tasted so good!

Wurzel Recipes

TOMMY BANNER'S SCRUMPY PORK
"e'll put 'airs on thee chest"

For a delicious pork in cider, you will need some Bramley apples, sugar, cider (medium) scrumpy if available, or a can of Autumn Gold if not. Also some King Edward or Desiree potatoes, an onion, chicken stock (either homemade or supermarkets do excellent tubs of the stuff), left over gravy from the Sunday meal and white pepper (to taste).

Cut the peeled potatoes in half and boil for about 20 minutes in salted water, or until they are almost cooked through.

Slice the apples and onion, and puree with the sugar until you have a chunky apple and onion sauce.

Slice the leftover pork, removing the majority of fat, place in a greased dish, in layers, with the apple and onion sauce, rather like a sandwich without the bread.

Pour half a can of the cider over the layers, pop the potatoes on top and then pour over the stock and leftover gravy until about an inch of the potatoes poke out at the top.

Sprinkle the tops of the potatoes liberally with white pepper, place in a hot oven until they form a crispy lid.

Serve with either fresh vegetables, or 'a girt dollop' of processed peas.

PETE BUDD'S TRADITIONAL ROAST BEEF
"assn't 'ee got any meat" said Pete, when confronted by a vegetarian platter at a well known Taunton Hotel

To enjoy a real Wurzel feast of Topside of beef, with onion gravy, roast potatoes, fresh vegetables and Yorkshire puddings, buy the largest piece of topside that you can afford, remembering those cold cuts for a later meal or snack. Rub the surface with powdered mustard, lightly season with salt and white pepper, place three or four small onions, which have been sliced in half and lightly salted in each corner of the roasting dish, cover with foil and then roast in a moderate oven, allowing 20 minutes cooking time for each half kilo of meat weight, plus an extra 20 minutes. For visiting Wurzels who prefer beef medium to well done, save the end bits, but leave the centre rare for guests who prefer it that way. About three quarters of the way through the cooking time, remove the foil, and expose the top of the meat, which then needs to be basted regularly until cooked.

Use King Edward potatoes if possible, boil them in salted water until they start to soften, then remove from the pan and drain the liquid into a bowl to use later. Drizzle some extra virgin olive oil into a roasting pan, place the potatoes in the pan, saving two large ones on one side. Mash the two you have saved, and then sprinkle them over the top of the potatoes in the dish, drizzling olive oil over the tops, the season with salt and white pepper. Roast in the oven until they are brown and crispy.

For the Yorkshire Pudding

110g/4oz plain, sifted flour
Half-teaspoon salt
1 large fresh egg
150ml/5fl oz each of fresh milk and water
Dripping or cooking fat
Sift the flour and salt into a large basin, break the egg into a saucer and then place in the centre of the flour, adding enough milk and water to make a beating consistency with the whisk, Beat well and allow to stand for at least 40 minutes. Allow 30 minutes before serving the meal to cook the pudding. Place the mixture in a greased baking dish, and place in a hot oven until the pudding rises and has a crunchy crust.

For the onion gravy

50g/2oz beef dripping (ask the butcher where you got your meat)
1 each of finely diced onion and finely diced carrot
2 rashers back bacon
2tbsp dry sherry
2tbsp red wine vinegar
50g plain flour
600ml/1 pt meat stock (The potato water and a couple of Oxo cubes will do)
1tbsp tomato puree
salt and pepper to taste

In a heavy based saucepan melt the dripping, add the onion, carrot and bacon then fry until light brown, add the sherry and vinegar, cook for three minutes, blend in the flour to make a roux then cook for a further 10 minutes. Stir in half the beef stock to make a thick mixture, add the tomato puree and the rest of the beef stock, and then simmer for 30 minutes. Finally add the meat juices and strain through a non-metallic sieve to serve.

Try to steam the vegetables rather than boil them, and always remove the meat and allow to rest for at least 15 minutes before carving.

JOHN MORGAN'S FISH 'N' CHIPS
"When thee's live on thee own, fish 'n' chips goes down a treat."

Fish and chips never seem to taste as they did when they were served up in newspaper, and the vinegar used to dribble out of the corner of the bag, and down your trousers! Forget all that foreign food, French fries and the like - good old British spuds with a nice piece of cod is still the nation's favourite.

If you can't get to the fish and chip shop, try making them at home - using a can of lager, 4oz flour, four pieces of cod, a pinch of baking powder and salt.

Sieve the flour, with the baking powder and salt into a mixing bowl. Make a well in the centre and pour in the lager, mixing well with a hand whisk to make a smooth, frothy batter. Remove any skin from the fish and cut into 4 equal pieces.

Now prepare the chips, using a nice floury potato like King Edward or Maris Piper. And here's the secret! Peel them and slice into big thick chips, and then boil them for five minutes in salted water. Drain well and set aside.

Heat the cooking oil to 190°C (375°F). Dip each piece of fish in the batter to coat evenly, and then lower into the hot oil. Fry for 4-5 minutes or until crisp and golden. Drain on absorbent kitchen paper, and then keep hot in a low oven.

Turn up the heat and plunge your dried, pre-boiled chips, into the hot fat, and cook until golden brown.

JAI HOWE'S SUNDAY TEAS
"A girt dollop of cream, and real custard, that's the stuff to give 'em"

Jai lives in Wales where they reckon the local cream is better than the stuff from Devon! Off duty Wurzels love traditional British food.

Sherry trifle, cakes and stuff

For Sherry trifle and real custard - you will need: -

1 Victoria sponge cake, sliced
300g (3/4lb) raspberry jam
1 wine glass of sherry
2 tablespoons brandy or Drambuie
Home-made egg custard (see below)
300g (3/4lb) raspberries
2 bananas (optional)
250 ml (1/2 pint) double cream
1 tablespoon castor (fine) sugar
Toasted almonds

Custard:

250 ml (1/2 pint) milk
150 ml (1/3 pint double cream
2 egg yolks
50 g (3 oz) castor sugar
Few drops of vanilla essence

Place the sponge in the base of a large glass bowl and spread with the raspberry jam. Mix the sherry and the brandy and sprinkle evenly over the sponge allowing it to soak in. Next add a layer of raspberries and sliced bananas.

To make the custard, whisk together the egg yolks, sugar and vanilla essence until pale and creamy. Heat the milk and cream together in a saucepan until boiling point then stir into the egg mixture. Once it is well blended, return to the pan and stir continuously over a low heat until the custard thickens. Pour into a dish and allow to cool. When quite cool, pour the custard over the layer of fruit, spreading evenly. Next whip the double cream, add sugar to sweeten and spoon on top of custard. Decorate with toasted almonds.
If you have managed to get some of that lovely Welsh or Devon clotted cream, why not try some homemade rock cakes to spread it on.

For about 36 small cakes you need:-

3 eggs
3 cups flour
1/4 cup milk
1 cup of softened butter
1 teaspoon of salt
3/4 cup of sugar
1 cup of dried currants
1/4 teaspoon of nutmeg
1 1/2 teaspoon of baking powder

Preheat your oven to 350 degrees.

1. Beat eggs with the milk.
2. Add the softened butter and continue to beat.
3. Combine the flour, salt, baking powder, sugar and nutmeg into a separate bowl.
4. Add the flour mixture to the egg, butter and milk mixture.
5. Mix it until it begins to get crumbly.
6. Mix in the currants.
7. Plop spoonfuls of dough onto a greased baking sheet, (about 2 in. apart).
8. Bake for 15 minutes, or until the cakes are a golden brown.

These are best served when still warm - smother with the clotted cream and then cover in jam until it drips over the edges.

Wurzel Songs & Speak

Wurzel Songs

Albert's Funny Farm (Tony Baylis)
On the other side of the Wurzels' single I Shot JR. Fairly light-hearted song sung by Gaffer Baylis.

All Fall Down (Pete Budd, AJ Smith)
Issued on a single - song about the effects of scrumpy drinking!

All Over Mendip (Adge Cutler)
This song describes a celebration day out on the Mendip hills involving nearly everyone in the surrounding villages. Issued as a single on Columbia in 1967, and then later in 1969 on the Carry on Cutler! album.

Aloha Severn Beach (Adge Cutler)
Adge's Hawaiian song, complete with Hawaiian guitar and backing vocals by the Wurzels. It describes "a little corner of heaven, down there by the River Severn".

Avonmouth Mary (Adge Cutler)
A tale of a lost love. On the second album, recorded at the Royal Oak, Nailsea.

Back Of My Old Car, The (Tony Baylis, Tommy Banner, Pete Budd)
Sung by Gaffer - describes the dubious goings on in the back of his old car.

Barcelona Blues (Adge Cutler)
Based on Adge's experiences when he spent some time in Spain.

Base Over Apex (Bob Barratt, Tony Baylis)
From the Golden Delicious album by the Wurzels. Song about a woman who keeps falling down.

Blackbird, The (Pete Budd, Tommy Banner, Tony Baylis)
An old West Country folk song. Bernard Miles in the Goon Show sang a version of it. The Wurzels couldn't find the original words so they wrote their own, found on the flip of Combine Harvester.

Bristol Song, The (Bob Barratt)
Written by Bob Barratt and on the Cutler of the West album. Contains references to many places in the Bristol and sung as a sort of "Clifton Calypso".

Cabot Song (Big 'Ead), The (John Christie, Pete Lawrence)
John Cabot going off to discover America.

Call Of The West (Sammy King)
From the Combine Harvester album, sung by Pete - about how wherever he goes, he still feels drawn back to the West Country.

Champion Dung Spreader, The (Adge Cutler)
Recorded on 2nd November 1966 at the Royal Oak, Nailsea, for inclusion on Adge Cutler & The Wurzels' first album. It was also the A-side of the band's follow-up single to Drink Up Thy Zider. It was Adge's answer to Lonnie Donegan's 1960 UK hit My Old Man's A Dustman and describes his old dad's occupation spreading dung far and wide with a "girt big blackthorn stick".

Chandler's Wife, The (adapt. Butch Kinsey)
Sung to the tune of The Lincolnshire Poacher, and previously recorded by Phil Harris, under the title The Thing in 1950.

Charlton Mackrell Jugband, The (Kevin Sheldon, Trevor Crozier)
The tale of what happened when the Charlton Mackrell Jug band hit the charts in the Farmers' Weekly.

Cheddar Cheese (Tommy Banner, Pete Budd, Tony Baylis)
The Wurzels' tribute to the most famous cheese in the world, originating from Zummerzet.

Chew Magna Cha-Cha, The (Adge Cutler)
A song with a Spanish twinge.

Chewton Mendip Love-In, The (Whitehead, Gardner)
A favourite with Bristol City fans from the album Carry On Cutler. Describes the goings-on at a "love-in" - an' if thee can remember what one o' they be, thee's older'n thee's look...

Chitterling (Adge Cutler)
A song extolling the virtues of that wonderful delicacy, otherwise known as a pig's smaller intestine.

Combine Harvester, The (Melanie Safka, Brendan O'Shaughnessy)
Parody of Melanie's hit Brand New Key, this rocketed the Wurzels to the pinnacle of the British pop charts in 1976, much to everyone's surprise.

Coughin' Song (Peter Knight)
Song about the evils of smoking, issued on a single - Pete Budd told me it was recorded as part of an anti-smoking campaign.

Crabapple Hill (Sammy King)
Issued on the album Combine Harvester.

Don Juan Of The West (Tommy Banner, Tony Baylis, Pete Budd, Ed Welch)
Issued on the 'B' side of Drunk On A Saturday Night - sung by Tommy Banner.

Don't Tell I, Tell 'Ee (Kevin Sheldon, Trevor Crozier)
The Adge Cutler laid-back attitude to life " LP.

Dorset Is Beautiful (adapt. Trevor Crozier)
Sung to the folk tune The Nightingale.

Down In Nempnett Thrubwell (Adge Cutler, Henry Davis)
The Wurzels recorded it after Adge's death on their 1976 album Combine Harvester.

Down On The Farm (Ian Whitcomb)
On the album Carry On Cutler.

Down Our Street (Sammy King)
Nostalgic song about childhood.

Drink, Drink Yer Zider Up (Roger Greenaway, H. Barter, R. Barter)
Features a wobble-board accompaniment.

Drink Up Thy Zider (Adge Cutler)
This song that started it all - written by Adge and in his words "the National Anthem of North Zummerzet. The original recording of the song was recorded as part of the legendary session at the Royal Oak, Nailsea, on 2nd November 1966, from which Adge Cutler & The Wurzels' first album was taken.

Drinking Man's Life, A (Tony Baylis)
The trials and tribulations of being an alcoholic.

Drunk Again (John Macey, Reg Quantrill)
The title speaks for itself!

Drunk On A Saturday Night (Pam & Chic Warner)
Actually the lads don't drink...much!

Easton-In-Gordano (Adge Cutler)
Homage to the village of Easton-in-Gordano in North Somerset.

Faggots Is The Stuff (Adge Cutler)
Favourite food for Zummerzet folk!

Farmer Bill's Cowman (Roger Greenaway, Roger Cook; special lyric Tommy Banner, Pete Budd, Tony Baylis, Bob Barratt)
Based on the 1967 UK instrumental hit I Was Kaiser Bill's Batman by Whistling Jack Smith. The Wurzels' version reached no. 32 in the charts in June 1977.

Farmer Jonesie's Travellin' Disco Show (Moody)
Originally a poem that someone (Mr Moody?) sent in to the Wurzels. They liked it and set it to music. It's about a farmer who runs a disco in his spare time.

Ferry To Glastonbury (Adge Cutler, Colin Thomas)
Bob Barratt describes it as "the answer to Glastonbury's traffic problem .

Five Foot Flirt (Cyril Tawney)
Written by well-known Devon folk singer Cyril Tawney - on the album Cutler of the West.

Folk Song (Ted Dicks, Myles Rudge)
About a plan to purchase a double bed...

Forty And Bone Dry (Geoff Betsworth)
A track on the "Eddie Stobart" promotional picture disc EP.

Freak-Out In Somerset (New words & music adapt. Bob Barratt)
Sung to the tune of the well-known rugby song "Four & Twenty Virgins".

Funky Farmyard (Tony Baylis)
"Everybody's havin' fun, down by the chicken run" in the Wurzels' funky farmyard.

Give Me England (Bob Barratt, Ed Welch)
The theme song from the film Confessions from a Holiday Camp.

Good Old Somerset (Tommy Banner, Pete Budd, D. Wright)
A homage to the Wurzels' home territory.

Gotta Have Tenderness (Mitchell Torok, Ronnie Redd)
A Country and Western song - also recorded by Glenn Campbell.

Haggis Farewell (Tommy Banner)
Tommy reminisces about his early days down in Zummerzet when he came down expecting to join a pop group in 1967, only to find he had to dress up in Wurzel gear as one of Adge's backing band, drink scrumpy and learn the local lingo.

Hark At 'Ee, Jacko (Adge Cutler)
About a teller of tall tales in the pub. Based on a bloke called "Old Dan'l Windell.

Harvest Of Love, The (Hill, Benny)
A UK top twenty hit for Benny Hill in 1963. Adge's version is fairly similar.

Hey, Come With Me (Tony Baylis)
Sentimental song about the West Country.

I Am A Cider Drinker (Hans Bouwens; new lyrics by The Wurzels)
Parody of the popular 70s song Una Paloma Blanca - this was the Wurzels' follow-up to Combine Harvester and their second biggest hit, reaching no.3 in the British pop charts.

I Couldn't Spell !!**&@&**!!(Wayne Carson Thompson)
On the album Carry On Cutler The song was originally a US hit for Sam The Sham & The Pharaohs in 1968, and has also been recorded by Fred Wedlock.

I Got Me Beady Little Eye On Thee (Pete Budd, Rod Owen)
About an owl in an tall oak tree.

I Hate JR (Ed Welch)
Song about the star of the US TV series Dallas.

I Keep Smilin' (Bob Barratt)
Issued as a track on the Wurzels' Golden Delicious album. Written by their producer Bob Barratt and sung by Tommy Banner. About a bloke who keeps on smilin' no matter what trials and tribulations he suffers.

I Love JR (Tommy Banner, Pete Budd, Tony Baylis)
One side of a single, on the other side I Hate JR.

I Shot JR (Ed Welch)
Issued as a single on John Miles' label.

I Want To Be An Eddie Stobart Driver (Jim Andrews, Tim Barker)
Issued on a promotional EP picture disc for the Eddie Stobart haulage company.

I Wish I Was Back On The Farm (Roger MacDougal)
Originally sung by George Formby in his 1940 film Spare A Copper it tells the tale of a country lad up in the big city and getting caught up in trouble.

If You Got Nothin' On Tonight (Geoff Stephens, Roger Greenaway)
Based on the Bellamy Brothers' "If I Said You Had A Beautiful Body Would You Hold It Against Me?".

I'd Love To Swim In The Zuider Zee (Stark, Christopher)
About a swim in a sea of cider!

I'll Never Get A Scrumpy Here (Ed Welch)
Story of a West Country man on holiday in France who realises he can't get his home comforts there - such as a hot meat pie, a pint of mild, and worst of all, a pint of scrumpy!

I'm The Captain Of The Dredger (Adge Cutler, Henry Davis)
On the album The Wurzels are Scrumptious!

In The Haymaking Tim (Adge Cutler)
A song about a lost love...

Jubilee Day, The (Banner, Baylis, Budd, de Sylva)
Her Majesty the Queen's Silver Jubilee.

Keep Yer 'And On Yer 'Alfpenny (Alex Glasgow)
A warning to young maidens of the evils that might befall them if they don't do what the title suggests...

Let There Not Be Light (Kevin Sheldon, Adrian Beecham)
The locals were up in arms when the authorities decided to install a light in the bus shelter - it was felt that this would inhibit their activities while waiting for the bus...

Little Darlin' (Maurice Williams)
The old 1957 hit by the US group The Diamonds.

Little Drop Of Home Made Wine (Rod Owen, P. Evans)
A rare song by the Wurzels which proves they don't only drink scrumpy and beer.

Look At 'Ee, Lookin' At I (Adge Cutler, Henry Davis)
An Adge Cutler song recorded by the Wurzels after his death.

Mabel, Mabel (Adge Cutler)
In Adge's words "a real love song from the old Arab quarter of Midsomer Norton" - a tale of "passion and pigs".

Market Gardener, The (Adge Cutler, Henry Davis)
What happens when a market gardener takes a young lady into his garden to show her some of his produce...

Marrow Song (Oh! What A Beauty), The (Siebert)
A horticultural song about a giant marrow.

Mevagissey (Pete Budd)
A homage to the village of Mevagissey in Cornwall.

Middle For Diddle (Kevin Sheldon, Adrian Beecham)
All about a darts match and the gamesmanship employed in order to make sure your team wins...

Mixer Man's Lament, The (Adge Cutler)
About the time when Adge worked on building the power station in North Wales.

Moonlight On The Malago (Adge Cutler)
The Malago is a small river or stream which runs through Bedminster in South Bristol.

Morning Glory (Guy Fletcher, Doug Flett)
The catchy chorus which was rewritten as One For The Bristol City and issued later, being adopted by BCFC as their theme song.

Mother Nature Calling (Tony Baylis, Reg Quantrill)
Issued on a single credited to Adge Cutler and the Wurzels, on the other side of Little Darlin'.

My Somerset Crumpet Horn (Tony Baylis, Tommy Banner)
About a strange instrument and what happens when a young lady comes around to have a go on it...

My Threshing Machine (adapt. Dwayne Detroit)
The sad tale of what happened when Adge took a young lady to show her his pride and joy - his threshing machine - in action, and the resultant mayhem when he let her have a go on it herself...

Nellie The Bionic Cow (Tony Baylis, Pete Budd)
A clever cow which can provide milk in bottles and cans.

Oh! Sir Jasper (adapt. Bob Barratt)
Old rugby song.

One For The Bristol City (Guy Fletcher, Doug Flett - New Lyrics by The Wurzels)
Rewrite of the song Morning Glory and adopted by Bristol City FC as their theme song.

Oom Pah Pah (Lionel Bart)
From the stage show and film Oliver!. On the album Carry On Cutler!.

Our Village Band (Tony Baylis)
From the Wurzels' compilation CD.

Pheasant Plucker's Son (Doug Taylor)
Take great care when singing the chorus!

Pill, Pill (Adge Cutler)
Song about the old Pill ferry.

Poor, Poor Farmer (Regan)
A tongue in cheek tale of woe about the financial hardships faced by farmers.

Pub With No Beer, A (Gordon Parsons)
UK chart hit for Slim Dusty in 1959. Written by Australian Gordon Parsons when he went into the only pub for miles around only to find they'd sold out of beer. In Adge's version it has a happy ending...the pub may not have any beer, but there's plenty of cider!

Rig Jig (Geoff Betsworth, Tommy Banner, Pete Budd)
Instrumental from the Eddie Stobart promotional picture disc.

Riley's Cowshed (Damerell, Hargreaves)
From the Carry On Cutler! album.

Rock Around The A38 (Tommy Banner, Tony Baylis, Pete Budd)
Tommy and Pete's favourite rendezvous at the Holiday Inn.

Sally-Army Teacher (Doug Taylor)
About a Salvation Army lady and the effect she has on the lads.

Saturday Night At The Crown (Joe Henderson, Bob Barratt)
Previously recorded (in 1968) by impressionist / comedian Mike Yarwood - both his and Adge's versions were produced by Bob Barratt, who co-wrote the song.

School Days, Young Days (Sammy King)
Issued as a Wurzels album track (on "Golden Delicious").

Shepton Mallet Matador, The (Adge Cutler)
Song about what happened to Jacko when he got back from his holidays in sunny Spain.

Sheriff Of Midsomer Norton (Dwayne Detroit)
Law and disorder at the edge of the Mendips.

Short Time Livin' (H. Spiro, A. King)
Song about making hay while the sun shines.

Shovel It Here (Tony Baylis, Tommy Banner)
Don't ask what is being shovelled.... just don't ask!

Sniff Up Thy Snuff (John Macey)
Life in a snuff mine!

Somerset Born And Proud (Pete Budd)
Another homage to Pete's native county.

Somerset Jigolo (Tommy Banner)
An instrumental played on the accordion by Tommy.

Somerset Space Race, The (Adge Cutler)
Somerset's entry into the space race. We'm off, off to Venus and Mars.

Sousaphone Sam (Bentley, Orchard, Shaw)
About a bloke who "wants to be one of the band".

Speedy Gonzales (Kaye, Hill, Lee; new lyric by The Wurzels)
Parody of the 1962 Pat Boone hit.

Springtime (Banner, Baylis, Budd, De Sylva)
Recorded for an Esther Rantzen TV show.

Sunny Weston-Super-Mare (Pete Budd)
The lads' favourite sunspot, where the tide is never in.

Sweet Violets (Cy Coben, Charles Grean)
On the second Adge Cutler album, recorded at the Royal Oak, Nailsea.

Tanglefoot Twitch (Adge Cutler)
A dance craze – Wurzel style!

Thee Cassent Kill Cooch (Adge Cutler)
The title refers to "cooch" (or "couch") grass, which has a reputation with gardeners as being impossible to get rid of - the song is about a bloke who never gives up trying to get what he's after.

Thee's Got'n Where Thee Cassn't Back'n, Hassn't? (Adge Cutler)
Flo & Joe and their little motor car which he has trouble manoeuvring in tight spaces.

There's A Spider In The Bathtub (Tony Baylis)
Written and sung - well, spoken really - by Tony Baylis.

Tractor Song (Idris & Evan Jones)
A Wurzelised edition of the Australian band The Mixtures' Pushbike Song, which reached no. 2 in the UK in 1971.

Tremble On (Roger Cook)
A Country 'n' Western style song.

Twice Daily (Adge Cutler)
This record partly owed it success to the fact that Twice Daily was banned from the air by the BBC for its references to pre-marital naughty behaviour leading to pregnancy and a shotgun wedding.

Two Milk Churns (David McDonagh)
An agricultural aria, as Adge might have called it...

Up The Clump (Adge Cutler)
Adge's rock 'n' roll number, complete with Tommy Banner's Jerry Lee Lewis-style piano playing.

Verger, The (Kevin Sheldon, Trevor Crozier)
About all the celebrities who visit the church and sign the visitors' book, curiously always when the verger happens to be absent.

Virtute Et Industrial (Adge Cutler)
Sung in "Bristol language", on the first album. Takes its title from "the old Bristol motto they used to have scrawled on the side of the buses.

When The Common Market Comes To Stanton Drew (Adge Cutler)
Adge's vision of what would happen to the Zummerzet way of life if Britain should enter the European Common Market, an event some years in the future at the time.

Who Needs Summer? (Ed Welch)
From the "Wurzels are Scrumptious" album.

Who Put The Bomp (In The Bomp, Bomp, Bomp)? (Barry Mann, Gerry Goffin)
This song was co-written and originally recorded by US singer Barry Mann in 1961 - Barry's version was a US Top Ten hit.

Wild West Show, The (adapt. Bob Barratt)
A song about the exotic delights of the Wild West Show.

Willie Friese-Greene (John Christie)
Song dedicated to the Bristol bloke who invented the movie camera.

Willie The Shake (adapt. Adge Cutler, Tony Baylis, Tommy Banner, Reg Quantrill)

A parody of the 1968 Scaffold no. 1 UK hit Lily The Pink on the album Carry On Cutler.

Wish I'd Stayed A Bachelor (Tommy Banner)

He assures us he doesn't mean it. Twice married Tommy, that is!

Wurple Diddle I Doo Song (The Village Band), The (Fryberg, Donnop, Kirsten)

The tune is an old German melody in 3/4 time.

Wurzel Rap (Lee Sheriden)

The Wurzels attempt to cash in on the 1980s rap craze.

Wurzel Rock (David)

Also known as Wurzelin' Time.

You Can't Kid A Kidder (Malcolm Mason)

A track on the "Eddie Stobart" promotional picture disc EP.

Wurzel Speak

Wurzel Lingo Explained Fer Furriners!

This page contains a dictionary of West Country words and phrases used by Adge Cutler and the Wurzels in their songs, patter, etc., translated into (more or less) English, which non-West Country natives or residents might find helpful.

Bissn't, Aren't e.g. Thee bissn't goin' far. Opposite of Bist (see below).

Bist, Are e.g. Thee bist = you are. See also 'Ow Bist below.

Cassn't Can't. See also 'N below for an example.

Couss Could.

Coussn't Couldn't.

Dollop Lump, quantity. Examples: a girt dollop of spaghetti; gave her a dollop o' girt big jollop.

'Ee Normally thee (=you); or he, depending on context, e.g. Hark at 'ee,

Jacko; Don't tell I, tell 'ee

'Em Them - see 'M.

Girt Great, big. Examples: girt dollop of spaghetti; put on thy girt big hat;

girt big 'ats 'n' cloaks; girt big blackthorn stick

Hassn't Haven't. See also 'N below for an example.

I Me, e.g. Don't tell I, tell 'ee; Look at 'ee lookin' at I

Jollop Medicine

'M Depending on context, means either am, him, or them. Am is used instead of are, e.g. We'm, They'm. 'M or 'Em is used instead of him or they, e.g. don'm = doesn't he or don't they. Sort o' confusin', en'm?!

'N It, e.g. Thee's got'n where thee cassn't back'n, hassn't? = You've got it where you can't reverse it, haven't you?

Oh Ar Means lots of things, according to context and intonation, e.g. OK, I see, is that so?,...

See also Ooh Ar.

Ooh Ar Popularised by the Wurzels (post-Adge Cutler) and became a sort of catch-phrase for the band. More of a sort of triumphant cry of Wurzel jubilation than an expression having any specific meaning. For prime examples, listen to songs such as Combine Harvester, I Am A Cider Drinker, The Tractor Song, Funky Farmyard, Farmer Bill's Cowman, etc.

'Ow bist?, 'Ow bist 'ee? How are you? A greeting.

Scrumpy Cider. Traditionally the Wurzels' favourite form of refreshment, rivalled only by beer in Wurzel drinking popularity, and therefore mentioned in many Wurzel Songs, e.g. I'll Never Get A Scrumpy Here, I Am A Cider Drinker, Drink Up Thy Zider, Drink, Drink, Yer Zider Up, etc.

Thee You. See also 'Ee.

Them They - see 'M.

They Them, e.g. staler than they = staler than them.

Thick The "th" in thick is pronounced as in this (as opposed to the "th" in thin). Means this or that, depending on context. Thick thur means yonder. Examples: Get up off thick mat; All thick sort o' stuff; What use were all thick learnin'

Thur There. See thick above.

Thy Your. Sometimes pronounced thee, as in Drink up thy zider (pronounced "Drink up thee zider").

'Tis It is. Similarly 'Twill = It will, 'Tain't = It isn't, etc

'Umman Woman. See Wi' below for an example.

Varmer Farmer. Many words beginning with "F" or "Ph" are pronounced as if they begin with a "V", e.g. Vorty-acre vield; Veet; Varmacist (although I never 'eard Adge say this'n)

Vernigh Very nearly, almost. Example: the garden's vernigh dug. Sometimes pronounced burnigh.

We'm We are, e.g. We'm off to Barrow Gurney. See 'M.

Wi' With, e.g. An 'umman wi' a few spare pound.

Zider Cider (see Scrumpy above). Many words beginning with "S" or a soft "C" are pronounced as if they begin with a "Z", e.g. Zummerzet = Somerset.

Zider Up Verb meaning to replenish with a sufficient quantity of cider, e.g. Landlord - zider I up or Zider we up!

Zummat Something, e.g. She upped an' zlipped, an' zummat ripped.